ANAPHORA

CATALOG   SPRING 2016

I0439072

Anaphora

CONTENTS

FEATURED TITLES

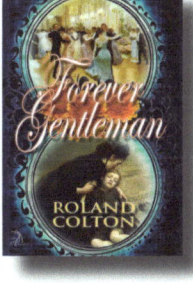
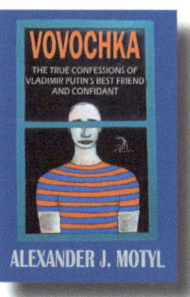

BOB VAN LAERHOVEN

ROLAND COLTON

ALEXANDER MOTYL

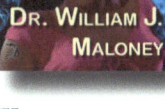

WILLIAM MALONEY

ANNA FAKTOROVICH

DAVID WALPUCK

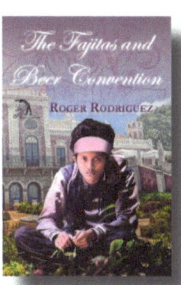

ROGER RODRIGUEZ

MARY JO PUTNEY

ALAN HOLDER

Biography

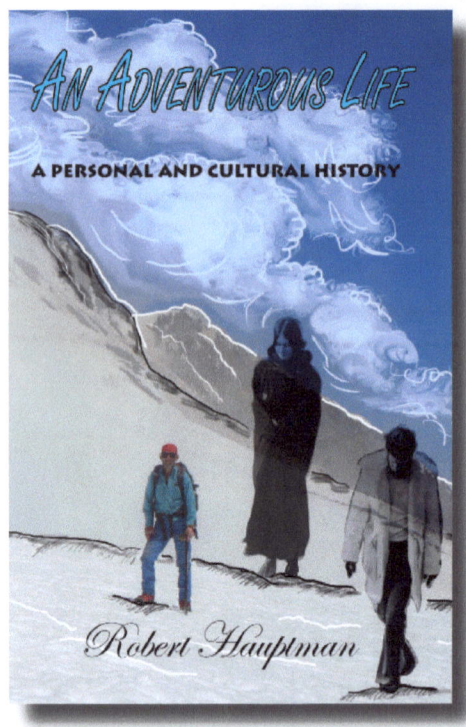

An Adventurous Life: A Personal and Cultural History ($15, ISBN: 978-1-937536-40-4, $30: Hardback ISBN: 978-1-68114-155-8, LCCN: 2013904196, 6X9", 142pp, March 2013): This book is the autobiography of an established academic, who also has a passion for climbing mountains and for enjoying the natural world, Robert Hauptman. Now a retired professor and editor of the *Journal of Information Ethics*, he reflects on the adventures he has had over the years. It's a great read for climbing enthusiasts and academics alike.

ROBERT HAUPTMAN is a retired full professor. He worked as a reference librarian and an instructor for a quarter of a century, first at the University of Oklahoma and then at St Cloud State University in central Minnesota, where he taught undergraduate and graduate classes in information media and honors program courses in the humanities and social sciences. He holds a BA in German, MA in English, MLS in library science, PhD in comparative literature, and PhD (ABD) in library science. He has some 600 publications in four disciplines: literary criticism, library science, ethics, and general interest. He is the co-author of *The Mountain Encyclopedia* (2005) and *Grasping for Heaven: Interviews with North American Mountaineers* (2011); his latest scholarly studies are *Documentation* (2008) and *Authorial Ethics* (2011); and he is the founding and current editor of the *Journal of Information Ethics*. In 2012, he did Lassen, the South Sister, and Adams. He climbs Vermont mountains, e.g., Stratton, Mt Snow, and Mansfield, very frequently. And he has stood on the high points of 45 of the 50 states.

A Berkshire Boyhood ($20, ISBN: 978-1-937536-52-7, $35: Hardback ISBN: 978-1-68114-147-3, LCCN: 2013951941, 6X9", 162pp, April 2014): Neither celebrity-gawk, "misery memoir," nor confessional melodrama, *A Berkshire Boyhood* is more reminiscent of such memoirs as Tobias Wolff's *This Boy's Life* and Emily Fox Gordon's *Are You Happy? A Berkshire Boyhood* will strike readers as a parallel universe to Gordon's book, her own story of growing up in Williamstown, as a privileged faculty brat and young girl in the 1950s.

ROBERT J. BEGIEBING is the author of eight books, a play, and many articles and stories. His novel *Rebecca Wentworth's Distraction* won the Langum Prize for historical fiction. *The Strange Death of Mistress Coffin* was chosen as a Main Selection for the Mystery and Literary Guild Book Clubs and is currently optioned for a film. His most recent novel is *The Turner Erotica* (2013), about both the secret and public life and work of J.M.W. Turner. His fiction writing has been supported by grants from the Lila-Wallace Foundation and the New Hampshire Council for the Arts. In 2007, Governor John Lynch appointed Begiebing to the Council for the Arts. In 2009 he served as the inaugural faculty members at the Norman Mailer Writers' Colony and as finalist judge for the Langum Prize. He is the founding director of the Low-Residency MFA in Fiction and Nonfiction, and Professor of English Emeritus, at Southern New Hampshire University.

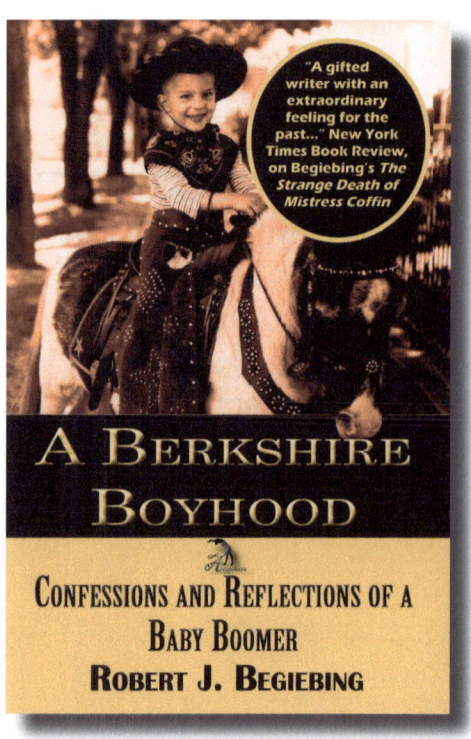

Domestic Subversive: A Feminist Take on the Left ($20, ISBN: 978-1-937536-67-1, $35: Hardcover ISBN: 978-1-68114-133-6, LCCN: 2014939989, 6X9", 236pp, June 2014): is an intimate, riveting memoir about the making of a political radical during the upheaval of the 1960s. It is both a personal journey and an inside look at political movements that changed the world. We see Salper first in fascist Spain, next in the heart of the New Left, the early Women's Liberation Movement, and the founding of Women's Studies. Finally she is engaged in third world liberation struggles in Cuba, Puerto Rico, Chile and the United States. As a Harvard-educated scholar, Roberta Salper was destined for a distinguished academic career. Instead she opted for a life of risk-taking, personally as well as professionally. Salper offers a unique look at marriage and family life within Spain's fascist dictatorship before she decides to "go it alone."

ROBERTA SALPER resident scholar at the Women's Studies Research Center, Brandeis University, and author of one of the early women's liberation anthologies, *Female Liberation: History and Current Politics* (Alfred Knopf, 1972) recently published two articles in *Feminist Studies*, "U.S. Government Surveillance and the Women's Liberation Movement, 1968-1973: A Case Study," (Fall 2008, volume 34, number 3) and "San Diego State 1970: The Initial Year of the Nation's First Women's Studies Program," (Fall 2011, volume 37, number 3). Highlights of her academic appointments include dean of the School of Liberal Arts at Southern New Hampshire University, director of Humanities and Social Sciences at Pennsylvania State, Erie, and resident fellow at the Institute for Policy Studies. She lectures widely on the history and practice of the women's movement, particularly Second Wave Feminism. Salper has a Ph.D in Romance Languages and Literature from Harvard University.

The Battle against Juvenile Bullying: The Plague of Child and Teen Bullying in the Schools and How to Stop It: ($15, 76pp, 6X9", ISBN: 978-1-937536-99-2, $30: Hardcover ISBN: 978-1-68114-116-9, LCCN: 2014957883, December 2014): "Dr. Leonard provides readers with a groundbreaking new perspective on the psychology of bullying. Using the concept of projective identification, Dr. Leonard masterfully explores the common misperceptions of bullying in order to demonstrate why most anti-bullying campaigns today aren't successful. Dr. Leonard's eye-opening text teaches us that it is only by first understanding the true psychological structure of a bully that we can prevent and put an end to bullying in homes, schools, and workplaces. Dr. Leonard uses a diverse range of real-life examples from her clinical practice in order to reveal some of the dominant characteristics of bullies, showcase the painful effects that bullying behaviors have on victims, and provide a insightful step-by-step process about how to successfully outsmart and stop bullies. Dr. Leonard has delivered a must-read book that will help parents, educators, and other professionals strategize how they can help put an end to bullies and support their victims." —Hailey Sheets, Communications Professor, Southwestern Michigan College

ERIN K. LEONARD has been a practicing psychotherapist for 15 years. She is the author of two books: *Adolescents with HIV: Attachment, Depression, and Adherence in Adolescents with HIV* (2008) and *Emotional Terrorism: Breaking the Chains of a Toxic Relationship* (2014). She has appeared on WGN and FOX affiliates in Dallas, Boston, Memphis, Atlanta, and Phoenix. She contributed a series of articles on depression and anxiety to magazines, including most recently to *Health* magazine.

Textbooks

Janet Yellen: Federal Reserve Chair: ($15, 48pp, 6X9", Print ISBN: 978-1-68114-203-6, EBook ISBN: 978-1-68114-204-3, LCCN: 2015915329, September 2015): The Federal Reserve (Fed), organized in 1913, is the central bank of the United States. The Fed is a governmental agency in charge of the nation's monetary policy and the chair of this institution holds one of the most powerful jobs in the world. Why? The United States has the largest economic system of any nation, at near $18 trillion. Janet Yellen was appointed Chair of the Board of Governors of the Federal Reserve System in 2014, serving as Vice Chair prior to the appointment. In 2014, Forbes ranked Yellen the second most powerful women in the world. The reader will learn about Yellen's early life, academic and professional career, and economic leanings. Terms and quizzes allow the reader to study the structure and functions of the complex Federal Reserve System.

MARIE BUSSING-BURKS: holds Master of Business Administration and Doctorate of Arts in Economics degrees. She is an Assistant Professor of Economics in the College of Business at the University of Southern Indiana. Bussing-Burks is the author of six other books: *Starbucks: Corporations that Changed the World*, *Influential Economics*, *Profits from the Evening News: Using Leading Economic Indicators to Make Smart Money Decisions*, *Deficit: Why Should I Care?* and *The Young Zillionaire's Guide to Taxation and Government Spending*. In addition, she has more than 30 magazine, newspaper, and journal articles to her credit.

Book Production Guide ($10, ISBN: 9781937536251, LCCN: 2012907287, 138pp, 6X9", October 2014, 4th Edition): Explains all of the steps involved in creating a book with the Anaphora Literary Press. It is designed as a tool for editorial, marketing and design interns of the press. It can also be used by publishing industry professionals who are working for other publishing houses, want to start their own press or want to self-publish their book. This book can be a great tool in editing, marketing and design college classes. The fourth edition of the *Guide* includes more detailed design and marketing advice, and a long section with marketing lists of book reviewers, libraries, and bookstores that hold readings. You'll also find instructions for making YouTube book trailers and Smashwords E-Books. Authors shouldn't set out on new book production and marketing ventures without reviewing the helpful information provided.

ANNA FAKTOROVICH is the Founder, Director, Designer and Editor-in-Chief of the Anaphora Literary Press. Faktorovich has also published two poetry collection, *Improvisational Arguments* (Fomite Press, 2011) and *Battle for Athens* (Anaphora, 2012), as well as scholarly books with McFarland: *Rebellion as Genre* (February, 2013) and *Formulas of Popular Fiction* (August 2014). Faktorovich worked as a full-time college professor for over three years. She has a Ph.D. in English Literature.

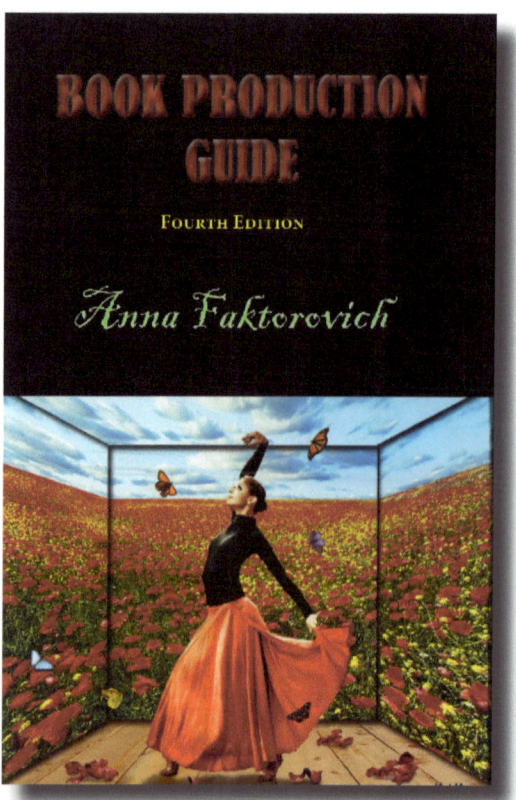

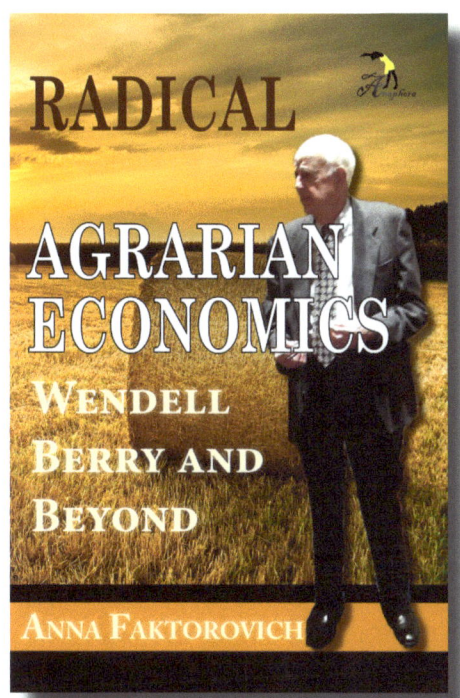

Radical Agrarian Economics: Wendell Berry and Beyond: ($20, ISBN: 978-1-937536-91-6, $35: Hardcover ISBN: 978-1-68114-125-1, LCCN: 2014917270, 180pp, 6X9", 7 photos, bibliography, index, January 2015): This is a comparative study of Wendell Berry's theory of New Agrarian economics in contrast with other agrarian proposals, as well as communist, capitalist and feudal economic theories. The argument for an agrarian world has both similarities and sharp contrasts with Marxist communism, industrial capitalism, and classic feudalism. Agrarianism can be seen more clearly when it is contrasted and shown as having existed in parallel with each of these stages of economic world development. As the world quickly grows in the direction of overpopulation and pollution, a re-evaluation is needed of the previously used sustainability methods that have kept humanity in balance with the earth for millennia.

"In strikingly honest terms, Dr. Faktorovich shares a chastened and sincere study of a utopian economics envisioned by a poet of the natural world. With her concluding image of knitting as an act conjuring warmth, nostalgia and consolation, as well as reminding us of the haptic poetry of tactile work, she delivers with picturesque detail and a hint of melancholy, an answer that is deeply true." —Catherine Corman, award-winning artist

"4/4 stars. A concise, well-written, detailed work of economic history and theory that situate[s] Wendell Berry and New Agrarianism in history, and considering the practicality of these ideas in the modern world. A textbook for the student of agrarian economics, [and] an elegant and accessible history of economic thought. Necessary for any reader of Wendell Berry, but also for thoughtful people from all disciplines with an interest in money, time, and the good life." —*OnlineBookClub.org*

Gender Bias in Mystery and Romance Novel Publishing: Mimicking Masculinity and Femininity: ($20, 298pp, 7X10", 67 illustrations and diagrams, bibliography, index, ISBN: 978-1-511888-90-5, $2.99: EBook ISBN: 978-1-68114-093-3, LCCN: 2015939747, May 2015): examines gender bias from the perspective of readers, writers and publishers, with a focus on the top two best-selling genres in modern fiction. It is a linguistic, literary stylistic, and structurally formalist analysis of the male and female "sentences" in the genres that have the greatest gender divide: romances and mysteries. The first part can be used as a textbook for gender stylistics, as it provides an in-depth review of prior research. The second part is an analysis of the results of a survey on readers' perception of gender in passages from literature. The last part is a linguistic and structural analysis of actual statistical differences between the novels in the two genres, considering the impact of the author's gender.

"A must-read for a mystery author like me, but also for every man and woman interested in the way we interact because art mimics reality… Or is it just the opposite… :) :)" —Bob Van Laerhoven, winner of the Hercule Poirot Prize

"Incredible amount of science—and not just theories that are convincing. The unbiased and very professional writing of the book and intriguing conclusions and statements found within the book make this a worthwhile and spellbinding read for feminists, people interested in gender, readers and writers. 4/4*" —LiteraryMagic, *OnlineBookClub*

"Informed and informative, thoughtful and thought-provoking, an inherently fascinating read which is strongly recommended to the attention of literary scholars and romance novel enthusiasts alike. Of considerable interest to authors of romance fiction. Especially and highly recommended for academic library Literary Studies reference collections." —James A. Cox, Midwest Book Review, The Writing/Publishing Shelf, June 2015

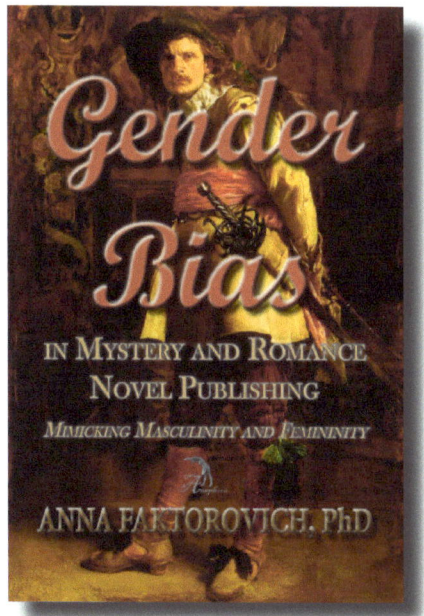

Persistence of Vision: The 21st-Century Film Criticism of Stanley Kauffmann: (\$20, 302pp, 6X9", ISBN: 978-1-68114-007-0, LCCN: 2015930072, January 2015): is a collection of film criticism by the late Stanley Kauffmann (1916-2013). Kauffmann's creative life spanned seven decades: starting in 1958 and continuing until 2013, he was a film and drama critic for *The New Republic*, *The New York Times*, and *Saturday Review*, among other publications. Along with Andrew Sarris, Pauline Kael, and John Simon, Kauffmann was one of the influential critics included in the New York school of twentieth-century American criticism.

In *Persistence of Vision*, Kauffmann discusses films from such countries as France, England, Mexico, Israel, Sweden, Austria, Netherlands, Argentina, Finland, Norway, Italy, Iran, Japan, Belgium, South Korea, China, Lebanon, Russia, Ireland, India, Greece, Chile, Romania, Turkey, Hungary, and the United States. Among the films reviewed are Michael Haneke's *White Ribbon*, Steven Spielberg's *War of the Worlds*, the Dardenne brothers' *Silence of Lorna*, Ron Howard's *Da Vinci Code*, Woody Allen's *Match Point*, Barbet Schroeder's *Our Lady of the Assassins*, and Nuri Bilge Ceylan's *Once Upon a Time in Anatolia*.

Educated at Tulane and Yale, **BERT CARDULLO**, the editor of *Persistence of Vision*, taught film and drama for many years at the University of Michigan, Colgate University, and New York University. His essays and reviews have appeared in such journals as the *Yale Review*, *Cambridge Quarterly*, *Film Quarterly*, *Cinema Journal*, and the *Quarterly Review of Film and Video*. He is the author, editor, or translator of a number of books, including *European Directors and Their Films: Essays on Cinema*, *Bazin at Work*, *The Films of Robert Bresson*, and *Playing to the Camera: Film Actors Discuss Their Craft*.

Survey of American Film: A Course Companion: (\$20, 300pp, 6X9", Print ISBN: 978-1-681140-89-6, EBook ISBN: 978-1-681140-90-2, LCCN: 2015904376, April 2015): consists of close, analytical, interdisciplinary readings of a number of important American films. All of these films are artistic "landmarks" in one way or another, or in several ways: because of their very subject matter; because of their style and technical or formal advances; because of the historical periods, social settings, or political backgrounds that gave impetus to their creation; and, ultimately, because of each picture's unique vision of the world. The author's approach combines formalism with historicism in the belief that films, like other works of art, cannot be properly analyzed and understood unless they are placed in social, historical, political, and cultural context. He decided to write this book as a companion text to his own course on American cinema, so that his students could read in depth about the films screened in class and could also be offered models for their own writing and research—in addition to topics for such writing and for class discussion, bibliographies, notes, movie credits, and filmographies.

"Survey of American Film… fulfills a real need, and it brims with original, often challenging insights, ever eloquently expressed." —John Mosier, Director of Film Studies and Professor of English, Loyola University of New Orleans

"Survey of American Film represents the kind of book I could well use—*will* use—in my own classes." —Andrew S. Horton, Jeanne H. Smith Professor of Film and Video Studies, University of Oklahoma, Norman

What Consumers Should Know About Food Safety: ($15, 94pp, 6X9", Print ISBN-13: 978-1-68114-221-0, EBook ISBN-13: 978-1-68114-222-7, LCCN: 2015955497, 20 illustrations, November 2015): is a collection of twenty-five true, eye opening, educational, and entertaining short stories about some of our worst food nightmares in and out of a retail food service environment. Highlighting the problems while offering solutions, this book is a must read for today's consumer.

The reported statistics on foodborne illness alone from the Centers for Disease Control and Prevention are cause for concern; the annual cost from medical bills and lost job productivity is estimated between 10 and 83 billion dollars. Every year there are 1,000 disease outbreaks, 48 million people (1 out of 6) infected, 128,000 hospitalizations, and 3,000 deaths are attributed to consuming contaminated food.

When people purchase food, there is a reasonable expectation that it will not make them sick. However, drug-resistant and emerging strains of bacteria, food recalls, cross-contamination, undeclared allergens, improper holding temperatures, pest infestation, inconsistent cleaning and sanitizing of food contact surfaces, lack of training, and infected food handlers are a constant threat to food contamination and personal liability.

DAVID WALPUCK has over twenty five years in the food service industry, is a Certified Professional in Food Safety (CP-FS) from the National Environmental Health Association, an Administrator for The National Registry of Food Safety Professionals, a Certified Food Safety Instructor, member of the International Association for Food Protection, a published author, and has fifteen plus years of experience in auditing, consulting, training development, and teaching.

How to See Beauty in Life: An Artistic Approach to Happier Living: ($15, 100pp, 6X9", Print ISBN: 978-1-68114-205-0, EBook ISBN: 978-1-68114-206-7, LCCN: 2015915439, March 2016): The ability to experience beauty in life is normal and natural. Unfortunately, few people are able to experience it due to the difficulties and personal issues in our lives. This book is about recognizing these problems and providing solutions so that life can be experienced in its natural and most beautiful state. Music is beauty. I have been a professional musician most of my life; therefore I have a great well of information to draw from. This book will open your mind to the unlimited sources of beauty available by taking you through an intensive journey into beliefs, the inner world of perception, the nature of reality and the nature of change, all done through unique methods and philosophies. I have had two major open-heart surgeries, the most recent one while writing this book. I hope you will enjoy it!

NORTH WOOD: As a professional violinist, he has worked with world famous award winning artists including Barbra Streisand, John Williams, Placido Domingo and many more. He has played on the soundtracks for Academy Award Winning movies and on over two hundred major motion pictures including *Schindler's List*, *A few Good Men* and *Mrs. Doubtfire*. He has also performed with nationally recognized orchestral ensembles. As a professional keynote speaker, North Wood has given keynote presentations to countless corporations and associations including New York Life, Kaiser Permanente, Century 21 and many more. North Wood is an author, teacher and has hosted his own cable television program discussing his techniques regarding the nature of talent and achievement. He is also a member of eight major speakers Bureaus.

Website: north-wood.com.

Diseases, Disorders and Diagnoses of Historical Individuals: ($20, 194pp, 6X9", ISBN: 978-1-68114-192-3, $2.99; EBook ISBN: 978-1-68114-193-0, LCCN: 2015947981, August 2015): Oftentimes, people look at famous individuals and think that such people are exempt from the physical limitations that bind us all as humans. Unfortunately, many times celebrities themselves think this is true. A stark reminder of this is the effects of substance misuse that have claimed the lives of too many young, otherwise healthy, luminaries in the prime of their lives. This book provides a background on each disorder or disease and, in so doing, shows the real humanity of the individual. Such is the case with baseball icon Lou Gehrig who was newly diagnosed with ALS, but truthfully believed that he was still the luckiest man on the face of the Earth. Little known facts are provided which enables the reader to feel like the subject has come alive as a real flesh-and-blood person from the pages of a history book. A never before seen letter from General George Patton is presented. In this letter, General Patton describes the author's uncle as "brave." Why did Patton have a near obsession with bravery—both that of his soldiers and himself?

Dr. William J. Maloney is a clinical associate professor at New York University College of Dentistry. He is a fellow of the Academy of Dentistry International, the New York Academy of Medicine, the Royal Society of Medicine and the Pierre Fauchard Academy. Dr. Maloney is the author of over 270 professional publications. He has also been presented with the Award of Excellence from The Floating Hospital of New York City. He has also been inducted into various prestigious organizations and societies, such as The New York Academy of Medicine and The Royal Society of Medicine.

Judas Was a Bishop: An Old Man in His Reforming Catholic Church: ($25, 330pp, 6X9", Print ISBN: 978-1-68114-211-1, EBook ISBN: 978-1-68114-212-8, LCCN: 2015916077, November 2015): The author, a practicing Roman Catholic, was confronted in 2002 with a leadership crisis in the church. Decades of horrendous clergy sexual abuse of children was accompanied by an even more momentous hierarchical betrayal in the cover-up of the crimes. The basic determinants of the current church crisis are, first, the sacred hierarchism of church structure and, second, the culture of clericalism that flows from it. The book also reflects on the lived Catholic life, contrasting the life of the priesthood and the life of marriage and family. The approach is at once narrative, historical-critical, and ecclesiological. The basic existential issue is "Why am I still a Catholic, and, indeed, why is anyone?"

"…Powerful, absorbing memoir, by turns angry, funny, engaging and painfully candid… Offers radical proposals for reform." —Michael Lacey (Oxford University Press)

"About the traumatic spiritual struggle with celibacy with which both Augustine and Merton were familiar. Finds God as a continuing presence, not at the end of his tale but in the twists and turns, the agonies and ecstasies, of his life journey." —Darrell Fasching, Professor Emeritus of Religious Studies, University of South Florida

William M. Shea graduated from the Columbia University in 1973. He taught at three universities and two colleges over his forty year career, was a resident fellow at the Smithsonian and at St. John's University in Collegeville. He held the chairmanship at Saint Louis University, and the directorship at the College of the Holy Cross, when he retired in 2008. His most recent book is *The Lion and the Lamb: Evangelicals and Catholics in America* (Oxford UP).

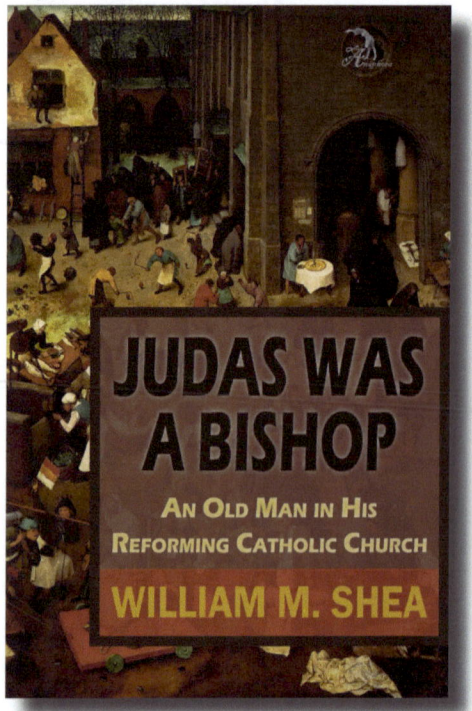

100 Years of the Federal Reserve ($15, ISBN: 978-1-937536-17-6, $30: Hardcover ISBN: 978-1-68114-175-6, LCCN: 2011945786, HG2563 .B83 2012, 6X9", 70pp, December 2011): Finally a book about the Federal Reserve targeted for young readers. This book should help middle, high school and introductory college students understand the U.S. economy and society better at a time when recessions, bank failures, and the growing deficit are regularly in the news. The book celebrates the 100th anniversary of the American Federal Reserve system.

MARIE BUSSING-BURKS: holds Master of Business Administration and Doctorate of Arts in Economics degrees. She is an Assistant Professor of Economics in the College of Business at the University of Southern Indiana. Bussing-Burks is the author of six other books: *Starbucks: Corporations that Changed the World*, *Money for Minors: A Student's Guide to Economics*, *Influential Economics*, *Profits from the Evening News: Using Leading Economic Indicators to Make Smart Money Decisions*, *Deficit: Why Should I Care?* and *The Young Zillionaire's Guide to Taxation and Government Spending*. In addition, she has more than 30 magazine, newspaper, and journal articles to her credit.

The Encyclopedic Philosophy of Michel Serres: Writing The Modern World and Anticipating the Future: ($20, 280pp, 6X9", ISBN-13: 978-1-68114-234-0, August 2016): This monograph represents the first comprehensive study dedicated to the interdisciplinary French philosopher Michel Serres. As the title of this project unequivocally suggests, Serres's prolific body of work paints a rending portrait of what it means for a sentient being to live in the modern world. This book reflects Serres's profound conviction that "philosopher c'est anticiper"/ 'to philosophize (about something) is to anticipate' ("Philosophie Magazine"). According to Serres, a philosopher is someone who possesses an extremely broad base of knowledge coupled with the uncanny ability to envision what might transpire based upon his or her astute observations concerning phenomena that are already starting to unfold in a given society. From 1968 to the present, Serres has been generating forceful, "prophetic" visions in his works that mingle philosophy, religion, theology, contemporary science, and literature.

KEITH MOSER is Associate Professor of French at Mississippi State University. He is the author of four other books including *A Practical Guide to French Harki Literature*, *J.M.G. Le Clézio: A Concerned Citizen of the Global Village*, *J.M.G. Le Clézio dans la forêt des paradoxes* (co-editor with Bruno Thibault), and *'Privileged Moments' in the Novels and Short Stories of J.M.G. Le Clézio: His Contemporary Development of a Traditional French Literary Device*. Moser has also contributed approximately forty essays to peer-reviewed publications such as *The French Review*, *The International Journal of Francophone Studies*, *Modern Language Review*, *French Cultural Studies*, *Forum for Modern Language Studies* (Oxford UP), *Interdisciplinary Studies in Literature and Environment* (Oxford UP), and *Pennsylvania Literary Journal*.

Novels

The Fajitas and Beer Convention: ($20, 152pp, 6X9", ISBN: 978-1-937536-94-7, $35: Hardcover ISBN: 978-1-68114-120-6, LCCN: 2014954338, October 2014): The story begins with the passing of little Manolo's mother. She left instructions with their ranch hand, Salvador, to deliver Manolo to their only family in the northern part of Mexico. Along the way, Manolo and Salvador encounter great adventures including a sinister drunk, a deceiving carnival owner, a magician, and the beautiful Paloma. The adventure does not end in northern Mexico! When Manolo and Salvador accidentally enter the United States on a train, they find themselves walking the streets of an American border town. Here they come across a wealthy neighborhood where ten Mexican gardeners are preparing to have a social. They explain that they all work for wealthy men, who are using the funds from their businesses to take vacations, meanwhile writing these off as, "conventions." So, every time their bosses leave, they use their houses to have their own "conventions" with fajitas and beer. Each of the men tells a tale during one of these socials, each with its own plot, moral lesson, and satire.

ROGER RODRIGUEZ is a professor of Sociology at Texas A&M International University and Lone Star College. He teaches writing and literature.

ROLAND COLTON was awarded a bachelor's degree from the University of Utah and a juris doctorate from the University of San Diego School of Law. He has had a long career as a litigator and trial attorney. Trained in his youth as a classical pianist, he is a frequent performer at public and private gatherings. He also possesses a passion for architecture and the French language. Colton lives with his family in Southern California and France.

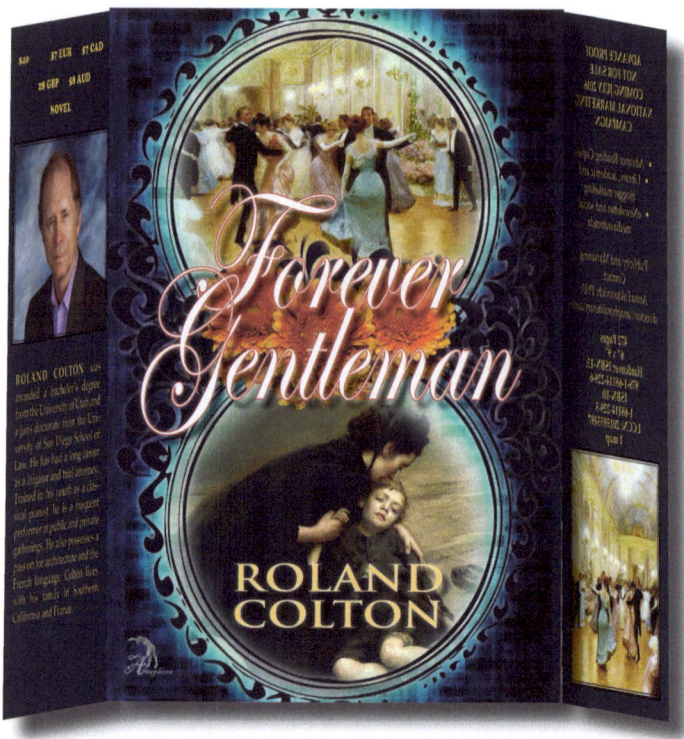

Forever Gentleman: ($40, cloth hardcover, 472pp, 6X9"; ISBN: 978-1-68114-229-6; Edited by Sofia Nehlawi; July 2016): Written in a nineteenth-century style, a sweeping saga of suspense, romance, mystery, and music. Travel back in time and experience Victorian London at its best and worst—a city of beauty and brilliance, and a city steeped in filth and despair. Meet Nathan Sinclair, a struggling young architect and gifted pianist who lives in two vastly different worlds, mingling in high society while dwelling in suffocating debt and poverty. While performing at a gathering of London's elite, Nathan meets Jocelyn Charlesworth, a breathtakingly beautiful but temperamental celebrity heiress. He is smitten, though she publicly humiliates him; their paths will intersect again in a most shocking manner.

Meanwhile, Nathan makes the acquaintance of Regina Lancaster, a woman of remarkable inner beauty, despite her pedestrian appearance. He must decide whether to follow his heart and pursue Regina, or flee England altogether to avoid imprisonment from a miserly creditor. In his darkest hour, Nathan is offered a tantalizing proposition that might change everything, but that comes at considerable risk. Nathan must play his role perfectly, or he may lose his reputation, livelihood, and very life to the powerful echelons of Victorian society. Full of unexpected twists and turns, the book races towards a thrilling climax that will determine Nathan's ultimate destiny.

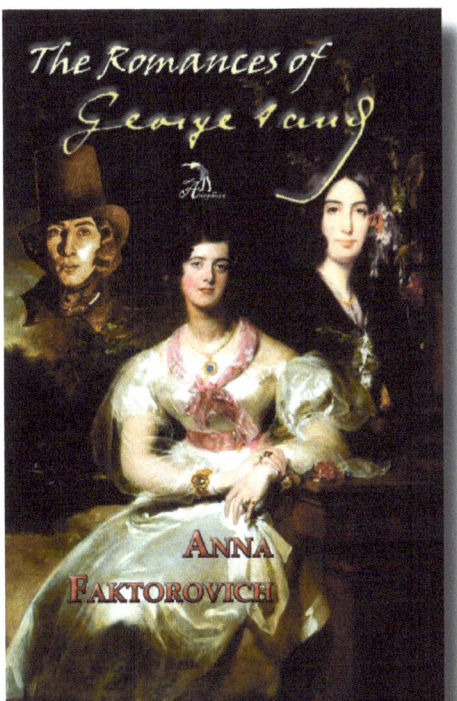

The Romances of George Sand (Paperback: $20, ISBN: 978-1-937536-68-8; Hardback: $40, 978-1-937536-69-5; EBook: $10, ISBN: 978-1-937536-78-7; 252pp, 6X9", LCCN: 2014908816, 23 illustrations, September 12, 2014): takes the heroine from a childhood in the aristocracy amidst the Napoleonic Wars, to an unhappy early marriage and eventual divorce, to her careers as a country doctor, pharmacist, lawyer, and most successfully as a romance novelist. George gets involved in violent, political revolutions of her time, including the July and June Revolutions and the 1848 Revolution; in the latter, she served as the unofficial Minister of Propaganda. The story is full of military battles, *coup d'etat* maneuvers, duels, malevolent plots, infidelity, artistic discussions, monumental legal cases, and reflections on the nature of love, family, romance, rebellion, and femininity. Historically contested stories are depicted, such as the lesbian affair George had with Marie Dorval and the identity of the real father of her second child.

"What a read! Not lacking in action and very imaginative." -Belinda Jack, author of *George Sand: A Woman's Life Writ Large* and Professor, University of Oxford

A "pleasing to read for readers of literary historical fiction and scholars alike… a complex and exquisitely researched novel that gets you hooked after a few pages… This is not a light historical novel but an elaborate story about a feminist *avant la letter…*" —Bob Van Laerhoven, Author of critically acclaimed, *Baudelaire's Revenge* (Pegasus Books)

"A must-read for scholars who will understand the numerous insider jokes and for women interested in the historical pioneers of feminism." —Rosie Rosenzweig, Resident Scholar, Brandeis University

The Battle for Democracy: ($20, 236pp, 6X9", 16 illustrations, reader's guide, Print ISBN: 978-1-68114-223-4, EBook: $2.99: ISBN: 978-1-68114-224-1, LCCN: 2015917681, May, 2016): The events depicted incorporate historical incidents to create an alternate history of a violent anti-corruption rebellion in the fictional town of Sparta, Tennessee, in the aftermath of World War II. It is based in part on the rebellion by veterans against the Mayor's office in Athens, Tennessee, as well as on the Chicago Haymarket Riot. In Sparta, thousands of veterans return to the States from the War, and are confronted by crippling corruption, as they attempt to drink away the trauma of the War. Faced with bribes and a heap of misdemeanor tickets, the GIs try to retaliate by aggressively supporting the Democratic ticket, but soon discover that elections are not won by voters in Sparta. The Sheriff and his army of untrained deputies go on a killing spree, as they work to steal the election, until the Democrats are compelled to pick up arms to defend their lives and their civil rights.

"A riveting account of corruption in politics from the interesting mindset of disgruntled post-war veterans. A combination that will intrigue readers throughout the story." —David Walpuck, Administrator for the National Registry of Food Safety Professionals

"Illuminates a little-known but highly representative incident in American labor history. A timely reminder that the greatest threats to democracy come not from abroad but from our homegrown ideologues and zealots, whether of party, creed, or avarice." —Robert Begiebing, founding director of the Low-Residency MFA in Fiction and Nonfiction, and Professor of English Emeritus at Southern New Hampshire University

Secrets of Gray Lake: ($20, 190pp, 6X9", ISBN: 978-1-68114-003-2, $35: Hardcover ISBN: 978-1-68114-112-1, LCCN: 2014922510, May 2015): Journalist Jenna Harris strives to write her way out of a quaint Great Lakes town and onto the staff of a major newspaper. The town and its people tug back—with old secrets, an endearing ethnic culture, and a lively group of 20-somethings sorting out life in the wake of the loose and experimental 1970s.

"*Secrets of Gray Lake* is a haunting story that creates its own half-familiar, half-exotic world in a small town in a 'far, cold corner of Pennsylvania.' Heroine Jenna is a features writer whose personal investigations take place in a world not absolutely fit for print, at any rate not in a small town newspaper. Drawn to a house-next-door of free-wheeling young people and their charismatic leader, Jenna is drawn *into* a life that skims the edge of sexual and nautical adventure. How much and how dangerously the history of the lake infuses its present is a secret that may never be adequately understood, but its pursuit makes for a story of recurrent and illuminating surprises." —Janet Burroway, *Writing Fiction, Losing Tim*

REBECCA **D**UNCAN is professor of English at Meredith College in Raleigh, North Carolina. She studied creative writing and literature at Florida State University and earned a Ph.D in British literature. Her publications include non-fiction essays, poetry, flash fiction and scholarly work on contemporary film and literature. Research and teaching opportunities have led her to Morocco, Bolivia, Mexico and Italy, as well as her homeland in the Great Lakes region of the United States. Among her scholarly achievements, she co-edited *Voices of Moroccan Youth*.

The Code ($15, ISBN: 978-1-937536-79-4, $30: Hardcover ISBN: 978-1-68114-132-9, $2.99: Kindle, LCCN: 2014945159, 6X9", 126pp, July 2014): When Abe Josef gets arrested for assaulting a college student and loses his scholarship to prestigious Tower University he wants to blow up the entire city. Since the "suits" from Tower think Abe's capable of violence he plans to become their worst nightmare. But, gangsters prove even less loyal than PhDs and he ends up facing years in prison for manslaughter. Abe's only allies come from unexpected places, an over-looked classmate, a small posse of street-writers, an ancient letter, and his own family.

PATRICIA **S**WEET: earned a BA in Writing from Houghton College and went on to publish several short stories. Later, she returned to school for teacher certification and taught English in the "hood" for twelve years, a city of her birth and has no inclination to leave. *The Code* is her first novel.

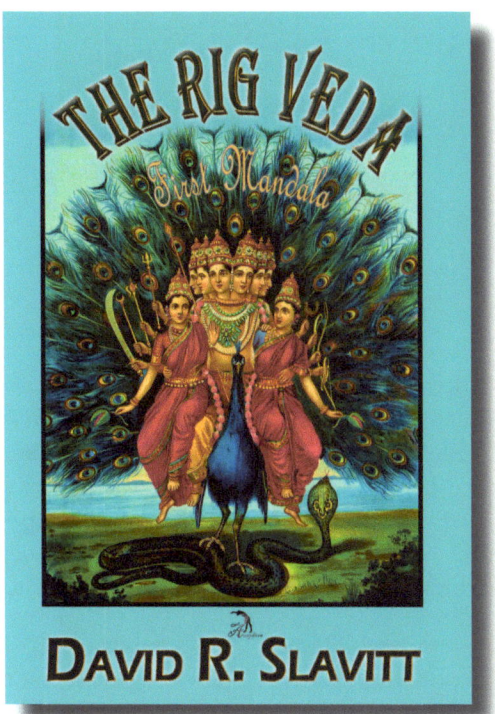

DAVID R. SLAVITT

The Rig Veda: First Mandala: ($20, 258pp, 7X10", Print ISBN-13: 978-1-68114-215-9; EBook ISBN-13: 978-1-68114-216-6; LCCN: 2015954420; October 2015): The Vedas are ancient books of hymns. There are four—the *Rig Veda, Sama Veda, Yajur Veda* and *Atharva Veda*—and they are the primary texts of Hinduism. They had an enormous influence also on Buddhism, Jainism, and Sikhism. According to Hindus, the text of the Vedas is as old as the universe itself. Scholars have determined that the Rig Veda, the oldest of the four, was composed sometime between 1700 and 1100 B.C.E., codified about 600 B.C.E., and was finally committed to writing around 300 B.C.E. The Rig Veda, composed of ten books, or Mandalas, each of which is a collection of hymns (suktas), is one of these "great books," but most people—even the well-educated—have never read it. It is very long and the previous translations are unsatisfactory. This book is an attempt to offer a succinct, accurate and readable translation.

"*Walloomsac*, Slavitt's latest work, may well be his bravest and most idiosyncratic. It is subtitled a *roman fleuve*, a river-novel, and its course indeed delightfully eddies from subject to subject… We learn about disease, the relations between men and woman, Shakespeare, disappointment, fonts and their origin, and the perils of misunderstanding. We are exasperated, dazzled, and confused, but always sure of our guide: our most underrated major American writer, and someone who combines learning with a sensibility truly—for once—conscientious." —Nicholas Birns, *The Tropes of Tenth Street*, January 20, 2015

Fabrications: ($15, Print ISBN: 978-1-68114-085-8, EBook ISBN: 978-1-681140-86-5, LCCN: 2015904378, 64pp, 6X9", April 2015): is a spritely love story that in its odd way recapitulates Henry James's *The Wings of the Dove*. A young man and a young woman are in love but don't have the financial resources they know they will need not just to be comfortable but to avoid the resentment either one would feel about having made a great sacrifice for their lives together. In James's story, Merton Densher married a wealthy young woman at death's door so he can inherit the money he needs in order to marry Kate Croy. Here, it is Nadine, the starlet, who marries the elderly producer with heart troubles, so that she and Abner, the writer, can look forward to a life of comfort and ease. Slavitt notices what James didn't, or couldn't in 1902—that the situation is inherently comic. And he has written a novel that is sprightlier than its model but, because of its humor, closer to the texture of life.

"David Slavitt has (herein) written a book about or for which it is impossible simply to write a blurb—a word, it might interest you to know, coined in 1907 by Gelett Burgess. (Did you think of a purple cow, just then?) The text itself is indescribably (deliciously?) itself. Like the Waloomsac River, it just keeps rolling along, taking the reader irresponsibly with it—laughing out loud again and again and again; marveling at its rapid wit (white water?), the wide breadths of its erudition, the dangerous shallows of its overt and covert cheekiness; marking the vertiginous depths of its, yes, wisdom. To make a long blurb short, I haven't had this kind of significant fun since I stayed up 'til dawn one night in 1962 breathlessly reading Pale Fire for the very first time." —R. H. W. Dillard on *Walloomsac: A Week on the River*

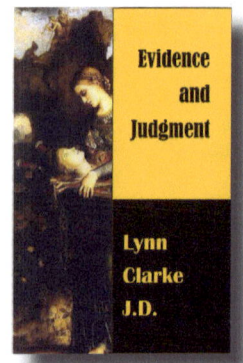

Revolution Time: ($20, 242pp, 6X9", ISBN-13: 978-1-68114-232-6, LCCN: 2016901305, February 2016): George Washington has three problems. One is the fact that the British have landed 20,000 troops to fight him on Long Island. The second is that the British navy is at his back, blocking any hope of retreat and the third is that two children, Eddie and Angie, claiming to be from the year 2014 have just been captured and brought to him by Lieutenant Collins. Eddie and Angie do not paint a hopeful picture of the upcoming battle. They claim to be lost, having been accidentally sent there by their eccentric Uncle Sol. Unknown to Washington, a British spy wants to kidnap the children and use them to help the British war effort. The challenge Eddie and Angie face is to stay out of the hands of the British and to find a way to get home. Uncle Sol and his assistant, Vernon, are frantically trying to find the children. The only problem Sol and Vernon have is that they are not sure of the exact time or place the children were sent. Fortunately, Vernon has a plan.

PAUL G. VARNAS has been a practicing chiropractor in the Chicago area for over 30 years. He has written many journal articles and several books about health and nutrition, including *Practical Magic* and *Fifty Ways to Lose Your Blubber*. He currently provides written content for Whole Health America and WholeHealthWeb.com.

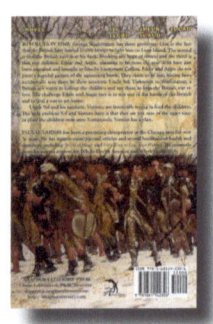

Walker's Father: ($20, 272pp, 6X9", ISBN: 978-1-68114-001-8, $35: Hardcover ISBN: 978-1-68114-114-5, LCCN: 2014959363, December 2014): The story begins five years after *Evidence and Judgment* ends. Jane Sidley, now Kaminski, struggles to cope with her husband Ansel's disappearance into booze and depression, when he literally vanishes after a flight from Heathrow.

Evidence and Judgment ($19.99, ISBN#: 978-1456501167, LCCN: 2011922235, 5.06X7.81", 244pp): The story follows Jane Sidley, a thirty-one year old moderately successful attorney, from the day she makes her last alimony payment to her rat of an ex-husband to the day he becomes a hero, falling from a tenth story window while trying to stop a terrorist bomber, sacrificing his own life to save Jane's child, whose paternity is uncertain.

LYNN CLARKE is Special Counsel for Bowles Rice LLP, Attorneys at Law in Charleston, WV. She has a JD from Harvard Law School and an Mst. from the University of Cambridge. Lynn currently practices in the areas of ERISA, employee benefits, executive compensation and retirement plans. She frequently speaks for civic and business organizations. She published her first novel, *Evidence and Judgment*, with Anaphora in 2010.

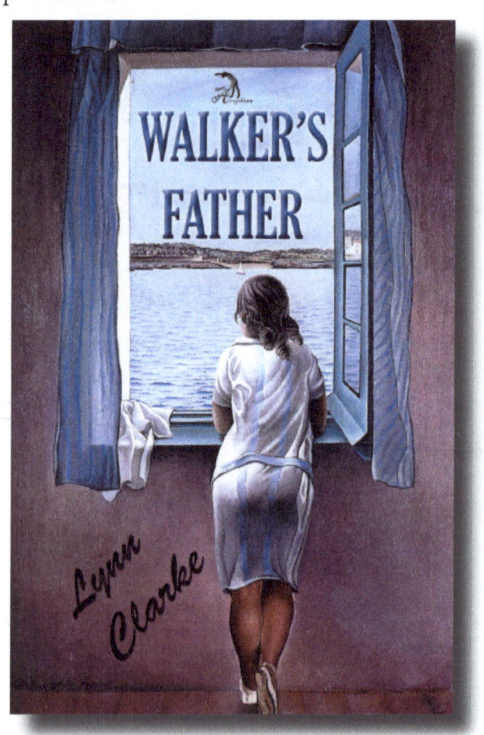

Where Gringos Don't Belong ($20, ISBN: 978-1-937536-81-7, $35: Hardcover ISBN: 978-1-68114-123-7, 174pp, 6X9"): Early in the evening of November 25, 2006, George Bynum, the protagonist leaves his Mexican novia Patricia among anti-government protest marchers in the city of Oaxaca, Mexico and returns to his apartment to finish a report for his employers, the Rural Development through Education Center. Before he can finish, his cell phone rings. "They're attacking! Killing! They won't…stop!" Patricia's voice rings in his ears. He rushes out, hoping to find her, but blinded by teargas from a federal police assault trips and has to be helped to safety. He and several others, including a young woman named Claudi Auscher, make their way back to George's apartment. Claudi, who defines herself as "a Mexican Jew gypsy bitch rebel" joins George in his efforts to reestablish contact with Patricia, who has been flown to a maximum security prison along with other innocent victims of the militarized purge. George and Claudi are based on the actual political and social upheavals that reverberated through Oaxaca from November 2006 through April 2007.

ROBERT **J**OE **S**TOUT'S books include *Hidden Dangers*, a 2014 analysis of the deteriorating ability of Mexico and the United States to deal with crucial problems such as crime, immigration and corruption. Previous books include, *The Blood of the Serpent: Mexican Lives*. A graduate of Universidad de las Americas, he has won national journalism awards for news writing and his fiction and poetry have been anthologized in a variety of publications, including New Southern Poets and Southwest. In addition to journalism assignments as a magazine managing editor, editor, newspaper columnist, contributing editor and copy editor and junior college instructor he has been a government account, theater owner, director and actor and sugar factory worker.

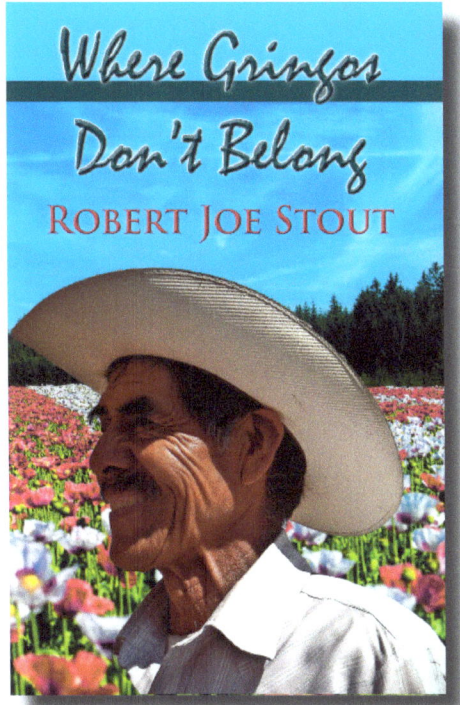

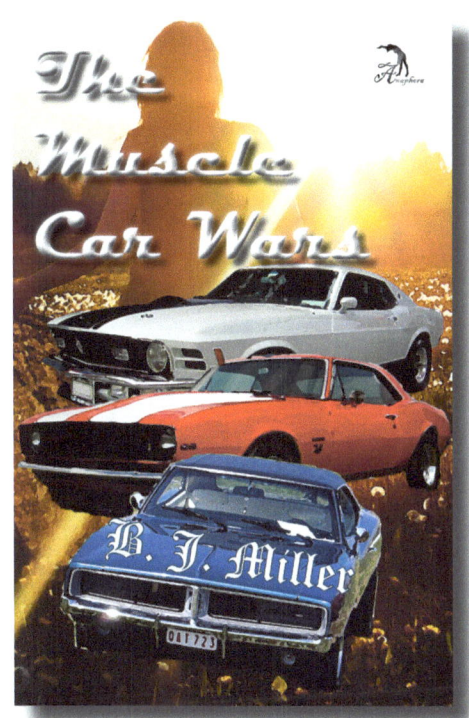

The Muscle Car Wars: ($25, 396pp, 6X9", ISBN: 978-1-68114-004-9, $40: Hardcover ISBN: 978-1-68114-110-7, LCCN: 2014922634, January 2015): tells the story of young man who suffers a traumatic head injury and while recuperating becomes involved in rebuilding and racing the powerful muscle cars of the 1960's and 70's. The book chronicles the major historical and cultural events of that era, including the Vietnam War, while weaving a tale of teen romance, amid tumultuous student protests and dangerous street races. Writing from experience, the author captures the essence of the time, putting the reader in the driver's seat of the greatest street machines ever produced, while retelling classic gear head tales, and providing a running commentary on every subject from religion, politics, drug use, the sexual revolution and romantic love.

B. J. MILLER suffered a severe head injury at fourteen, while working on a corn detasseling crew that left him with a hearing impairment. Miller spent his high school years rebuilding classic muscle cars. He graduated from Iowa City High School in 1974, eventually quit stonecutting and worked his way through college as a bus driver and handicapped student aid. He is a graduate of the University of Iowa, Idaho State University, and Drake University. He has worked for 28 years now as a teacher and librarian.

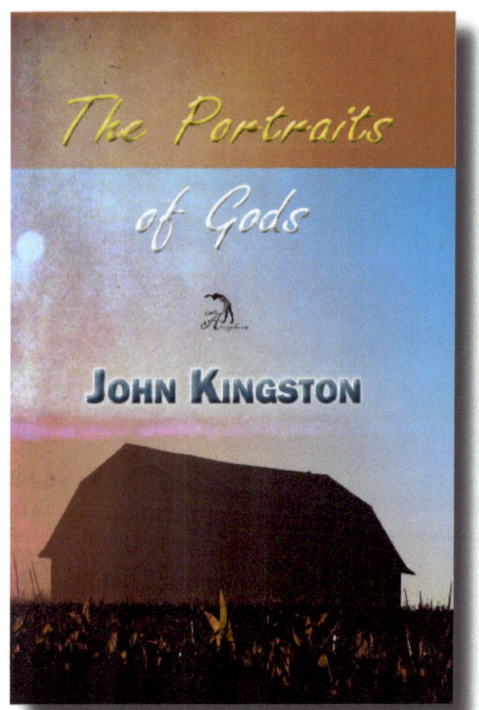

The Portraits of Gods ($20, ISBN: 978-1-937536-88-6, $35: Hardcover ISBN: 978-1-68114-122-0, LCCN: 2014951290, 6X9", 174pp, January 2015): forty-nine year-old Ethan Wakefield discovers that he is approaching retirement, and is distressed that he will no longer have an escape in work from his tumultuous home-life. Complicating matters, he possesses an extraordinary ability to recall specific events from any given date in his past with uncanny accuracy. It's this very ability that causes him to dwell incorporeally in the doorway between past and present, comparing the dreams and reverie of youth to the despair of his adult life. One day, during his commute to work, Ethan misses his exit. But instead of getting off at the next, he continues driving, setting into motion events that will force him to strip away his desensitization by pitting past against present, and will breathe new life into his search for validity and meaningfulness. Set in California's mythic Mayacamas Mountains, *The Portraits of Gods* blends beauty and symmetry of language to tell the tale of lost love and one man's struggle with the slow-acting poison of regret.

JOHN KINGSTON: is a prolific writer, with articles in the *Huffington Post*, *Blue Heron*, *Treasure Chest of Memories*, and the *Redwoods Society Writers' Cartel*. He has a degree from Michigan State University and resides in Lansing, Michigan. In order to support his insatiable writing appetite, he "moonlights" as a police officer.

Fireworks: ($20, ISBN: 978-1-937536-92-3, $35: Hardcover ISBN: 978-1-68114-121-3, 6X9", 180pp, February 2015): two women are thrown into the Hezbollah Israel war of 2006. Angie is thirty, a nurse from Kansas, in Beirut for the summer to get away from a broken heart. Zahra is a sixteen year old Shiite, on summer break and in love for the first time. Through terror, loss, grief, self-forgiveness and the workings of a local doctor, the two women move from despair to grace and to the long-awaited shore.

SARAH HOUSSAYNI was born in Beirut, Lebanon, she moved to upstate NY at the age of 25 to complete her training in Pediatrics. She lives in Wichita, Kansas where she raises two boys and is a clinical assistant professor at Kansas University. She has published *Narratives in Family Medicine*, *Survive and Thrive*, *The Examined Life* and *Pulse Voices*. She is a Writer's Digest Award Winner for Personal Essay, this is her first book.

"*Fireworks* illuminates the complexity of religious codes and cultural boundaries. From Kansas City to Beirut, Houssayni's characters navigate family tension, political unrest, and unexamined grief. This is a writer full of curiosity and courage." –Christine Hemp, award winning poet and NPR host, www.christinehemp.com

"This story could not be more timely. The breadth of Houssayni's empathetic imagination in *Fireworks* is impressive; the writing is sensitive to difference in the best sense." –Charles Holdefer, *The Contractor*

"Sarah Houssayni's *Fireworks* delivers a vivid and rewarding tale. From Kansas City to New York City, to Beirut, Houssayni's debut encompasses and transcends the known world through characters that are fully fleshed and deftly wrought." –Juliet Patterson, *The Truant Lover* and *Dirge*

Lombard Street: A Novel: ($20, 218pp, 6X9", Print ISBN: 978-1-68114-101-5, $2.99: EBook ISBN: 978-1-68114-102-2, $35: Hardcover ISBN: 978-1-68114-185-5, June 2015): Diving to the very depths of human feeling and then scrambling desperately to the surface for that last breath of air, *Lombard Street* weaves the riveting tale of a man's dangerous and emotional journey through marriage, addiction, madness, countless misfires, and across seas of broken promises from San Francisco to Singapore to Hong Kong.

"When I got home that evening all the finished paintings and drawings had disappeared from the apartment and the large Haitian canvas had been returned, though Janet made no mention of it.

"So perhaps this obsession had run its course and apparently she'd lost her passion for the whole Voodoo episode although two of Harold's books still sat on her nightstand in the bedroom. The less said the better about these seemingly unexplained things, I thought to myself.

"In the past some unfortunate things had happened to us, we didn't have children for one. And we had tried for years, particularly those first few years.

"She had suffered a devastating miscarriage some time ago, and that had forced a striking change in her manner though subtle at first."

BRUCE **C**OLBERT grew up in the Pennsylvania coal valleys and later served as a Navy enlisted man and officer, and then as a journalist, traveling the world. His short story collection, *A Tree on the Rift* (Lummox Press) was released in 2014.

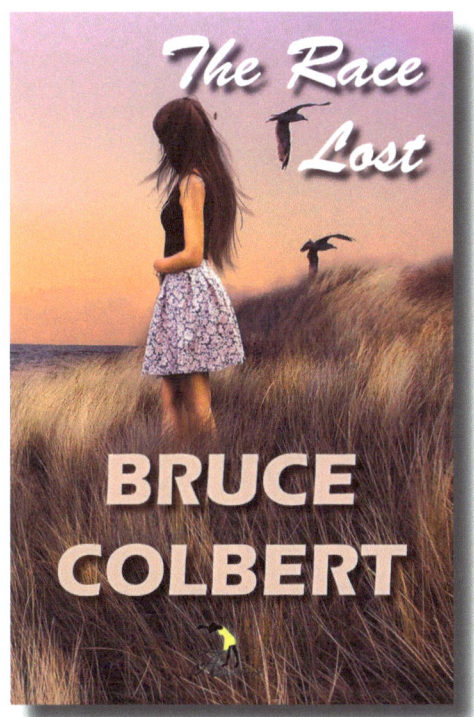

The Race Lost: ($15, 56pp, 6X9", Print ISBN: 978-1-68114-194-7; $2.99: EBook ISBN: 978-1-68114-195-4, LCCN: 2015948415, August 2015): Abundantly clear, this passage, begun in youth, and without fear or remorse, traces uncertain human paths like a blind man whose agile fingers uncover all there is to know with the lightest touch. Immeasurably rich, this interpreter offers open wounds and inexhaustible hope.

#17: Amazon Hot New Releases in Love Poems List

San Francisco Evening

Steep steps exhaust us so we're unready for the dragons

of defeated Chinese dynasties whose magic clutched a sinking heart

Drunk with nighttime incense, a sorcerer awaits as imagination's key unlocks the lacquered red apartment door, you're home, not yet…

Friday: A Novel ($15, Print ISBN: 978-1-68114-010-0, $2.99: EBook ISBN: 978-1-68114-091-9, $30: Hardcover ISBN: 978-1-68114-105-3, LCCN: 2015901689, 6X9", 108pp, May 2015): On an unassuming Friday, the lives of five people converge and explode in a small American town. A sister returns home to reclaim herself; a brother is pushed to the edge when confronted by a violent memory; a father rekindles a secret high school crush; an aunt questions her marriage as her husband's libido dwindles; and, the ghost of a local priest haunts them all. Told with a unique literary voice, *Friday* examines the languor and melancholy of the day-to-day life, and the exaltation when a choice is finally made.

MATTHEW R. K. HAYNES was a State of Idaho Writing Fellow in 2010. He earned his M.A. in Fiction and M.F.A. in Creative Nonfiction from Boise State University. While doing graduate work, his first novel, *Moving Towards Home*, was published. Subsequently, his work has appeared in several anthologies and journals, including *SOMA Literary Journal*, *O'iwi*, *Native Literatures*, *Fringe* and *Yellow Medicine Review*. He was been a finalist for the Faulkner Award in Nonfiction and Writer's Digest Award in Fiction, and, most recently, the Glimmer Train Award for Short Fiction. His collection of multi-genre writing, titled, *Shall We Not Go Missing*, has been chosen for the Wayne Kaumuali'i Westlake Monograph Series, and is forthcoming from Kuleana Press in 2015.

When Leaves Change Color: ($19.90, 7X10", 230pp, ISBN: 978-1-68114-190-9; $2.99: EBook ISBN: 978-1-68114-191-6, LCCN: 2015947749, August 2015): is an adventure based on the introduction of horses to the Plains Indians. Santiago Ortega was born to a wealthy family living on a sprawling ranch in the Spanish province of New Mexico. When the Pueblo Indians revolt against the Spaniards, the lives and dreams of Santiago and his family are forever shattered. Santiago embarks on a dangerous journey back into New Mexico to find a lost brother and to seek revenge on all Indians. Ouray lives in poverty with his Indian tribe in a desert on the high plains of Wyoming. Ouray's life unravels when hostile warriors destroy his family and capture the woman he loves.

JOHN BRADFORD BRANNEY was born and raised in Wyoming. He attended the University of Wyoming, where he received a B.S. degree in geology. During his career in the energy industry, John obtained an MBA degree from the University of Colorado. In 2011, he retired and pursued a second career as an author. John's passion and expertise in high plains archaeology has led to several books on the subject and over twenty-five magazine articles.

"Meticulously researched, brilliantly written, and clearly demonstrates a comfortable, first-hand learned awareness for Plains Indians lifeways and High Plains environments. Two sub-plots or themes are masterfully and skillfully coiled and twined and twisted like a Southwestern Indian basket… including a subtle open 'spirit-line' at the novel's conclusion… Of special interest to readers who have a 'soft spot' for the bonding between a young boy and his colt—a bond that provides a clever, opportunistic, unforeseen ending to the story." –Elmer A. Guerri, *Prehistoric American*

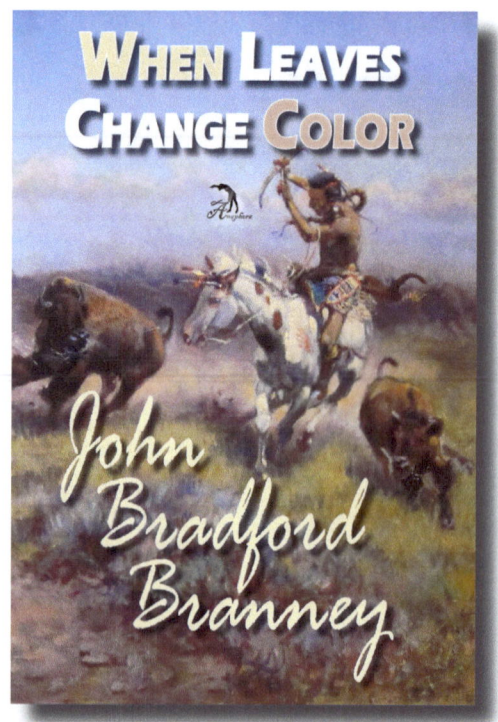

Vovochka: The True Confessions of Vladimir Putin's Best Friend and Confidant: ($20, 152pp, 6X9", Print ISBN: 978-1-68114-201-2, EBook ISBN: 978-1-68114-202-9, LCCN: 2015915059, October 2015): Welcome to Vladimir Putin's phantasmagoric world, where a heady mixture of Orthodoxy, socialism, imperialism, racism, homophobia, and Mother Russia worship defines and distorts reality. Vovochka is the story of "Vovochka" Putin and his intimate friend—a KGB agent with the same nickname. The two Vovochkas recruit informers in Berlin's gay bars, spy on East German dissidents, survive the trauma of the Soviet Union's collapse, fight American, Ukrainian, Jewish, and Estonian "fascists," and plot to restore Russia's power and glory. As their mindset assumes increasingly bizarre forms, Vovochka Putin experiences bouts of self-doubt that culminate in a weeklong cure in North Korea. A savage satire, Vovochka is also a terrifyingly plausible account of Vladimir Putin's evolution from a minor KGB agent in East Germany to the self-styled Savior and war-mongering leader of a paranoid state.

ALEXANDER J. MOTYL'S artwork has been displayed in shows in New York, Philadelphia, and Toronto and is part of the permanent collection of the Ukrainian Museum in New York and the Ukrainian Cultural and Educational Centre in Winnipeg. He teaches at Rutgers University-Newark and is the author of six academic books, many articles.

"Buy the Book: Russia's Macho Leader Exposed: Motyl's story succeeds on two levels: it overlays actual events with a slightly skewed fictional story, and it exploits the bombast of Russian officialdom by pretending to take it seriously. The result is a parody in the great tradition of free expression." —*The American Spectator*

"Drips with veracity, with the truth of today's Russia. Nothing funny here. The tsar has returned from the grave. Only a miracle can prevent Russia and its people from sliding back to its deep-rooted ways." —Myron Kuropas, *The Ukrainian Weekly*

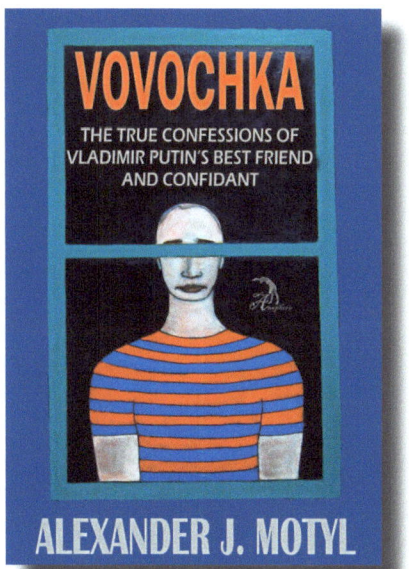

*Finalist in Gival Press' 2015 novel competition

Something Is Rotten in Fettig: ($20, 268pp, 6X9", Print ISBN: 978-1-68114-197-8, EBook ISBN: 978-1-68114-198-5; LCCN: 2015949531, February 2016): Told in a wry, understated voice, the novel satirizes the travails of Leopold Plotkin, a failing kosher butcher with a pathological aversion to conflict. After Plotkin commits an act that ignites a crisis in his Republic, he is propelled into conflicts with every branch of government. When he refuses the government's demands to undo what he did, he is indicted by a Secret Blind Jury, arrested by the National Constabulary, and consigned to the notorious Purgatory House of Detention, where he languishes next to a defrocked insane lawyer whose nocturnal machinations threaten to drive him crazy.

"…The uproarious novel is first and foremost a comedy, rife with absurdist humor…[e]nough jabs at law and criminal justice to make a point, all packaged in a courtroom drama that's pure entertainment."—*Kirkus Reviews*

"4/5*: You're moving along at steady clip, completely immersed in Plotkin's unwitting journey towards public damnation, and properly outraged by the irrational and illogical flavor of the evidence that's stacked against him. Delightfully satirical, the author takes a jab at everything from judges, to juries, to lawyers, to public manipulation and ignorance, oftentimes with hilarious results." —*Manhattan Book Review*, "Humor," Heather Clawson

JERE KRAKOFF was a civil rights attorney with the ACLU National Prison Project in Washington, D.C., the Lawyers Committee for Civil Rights Under Law in Mississippi, and a legal aid program in Pittsburgh. Website: jerekrakoff.com

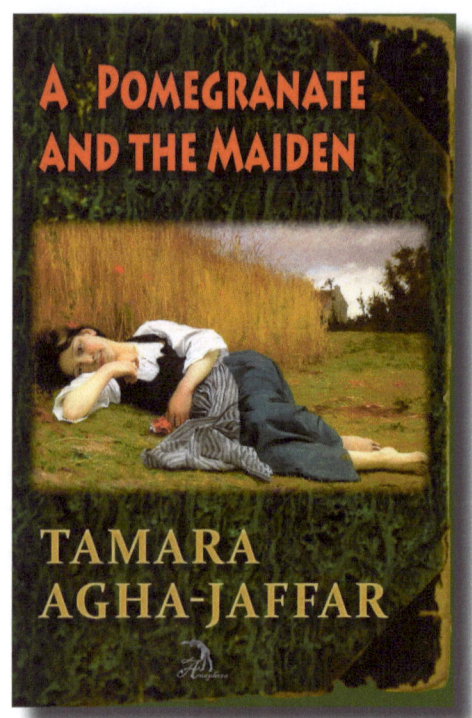

A Pomegranate and the Maiden: ($20, 198pp, 6X9", Print ISBN: 978-1-68114-209-8, EBook ISBN: 978-1-68114-210-4, LCCN: 2015916043, October 2015): is a multi-faceted re-telling of Homer's Hymn to Demeter. The many characters speak directly to the reader, presenting multiple perspectives of the same event. Among the voices we hear is that of the mother grieving for her lost child, the daughter struggling for independence, the father who tramples on a mother's rights, and the lover who resorts to nefarious means to win his beloved. Each perspective is deeply rooted in the character's psychology and gender. Woven within their narratives are stories familiar to readers of Greek mythology. Against the backdrop of our own culture, which still diminishes the value of motherhood and marginalizes women of all ages, these voices speak to us through the centuries and offer new ways of seeing the world we inhabit.

TAMARA AGHA-JAFFAR has a Ph.D. in English Literature. She has served as a Professor of English, Dean, and Vice President for Academic Affairs. She retired in July 2013. In 2004, she was named Kansas Professor of the Year by the Carnegie Foundation and received its CASE Award for the Advancement of Teaching. In 2010, she received The President's Call to Service Award for her volunteer work in the community. Her previous books are *Demeter and Persephone: Lessons from a Myth* (McFarland 2002) and *Women and Goddesses in Myth and Sacred Texts* (Longman 2004). Tamara lives in Kansas with her husband of thirty-eight years. They are the proud parents of a physician and an attorney, and the grandparents of a delightful young man who has just advanced to the class of Toddler Two. *A Pomegranate and the Maiden* is her first novel. Tamara can be found online at tamaraaghajaffar.com.

Who Is Olivia Green? ($20, 202pp, 6X9", Print ISBN: 978-1-68114-225-8; $2.99: EBook ISBN: 978-1-68114-226-5, LCCN: 2015919800, December 2015): Lawyer. Spy. Lover. Fighter. This debut thriller follows Olivia Green as she becomes all these and yet remains a mystery, even to herself. Lawyer: A young associate in a high-powered firm building a fledgling office in Augusta, Georgia. Spy: Recruited in high school to work for a secret organization that was formed after 9/11, an organization tasked with doing whatever it takes to keep the country safe. Their protégé, Olivia, surpasses expectations on her first assignment and moves onto her next mission, an assassination. Lover: From teachers to gym instructors, no man can resist her charm and fierce intensity. Fighter: Shady men lurking in the shadows get more than they bargained for from this CrossFit enthusiast.

DAVID HEATON grew up in Olney, Maryland and moved south to attend Georgia Southern University. He graduated in 1998 and began a career in law enforcement with the City of Statesboro Police Department. He currently lives in Augusta, Georgia with his daughter. He writes about anything and everything on his blog at http://dheaton.org.

Brandi de Talence (Editor) graduated from Appalachian State University in 2012 with a Bachelor of Arts in English. She lives in Raleigh, North Carolina with her husband.

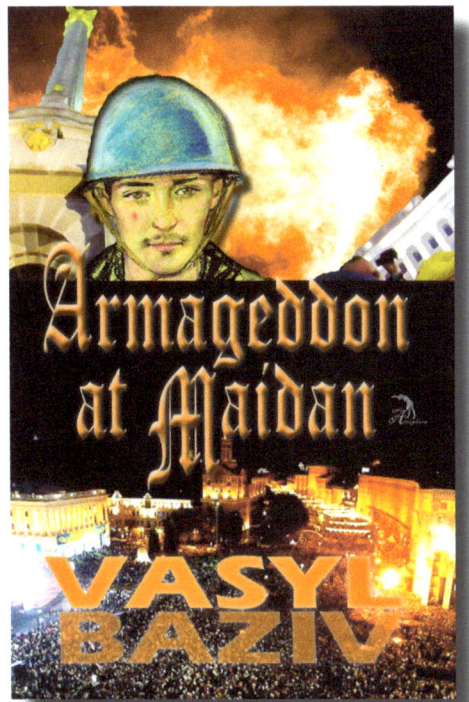

Armageddon at Maidan: ($20, 166pp, 6X9", Print ISBN-13: 978-1-68114-227-2, EBook ISBN-13: 978-1-68114-228-9, LCCN: 2015959445, 45 color photographs by Valerian Antonovych and Lesia Lutsiv, Edited by Kristen Noy, February 2016): is a novel-requiem based on real stories, heroes and monsters. This is the first fictional portrayal of the galactic-scale events in Maidan, in the heart of Kyiv, Ukraine that have left their mark on world history. The protagonist of the novel, Yarko, feels that he can no longer stay at home, as he watches the capital of his country being absorbed by the revolution on TV. He takes a leave of absence at the institute where he works as a researcher, and leaves his family, rushing at dawn to catch a train to Kyiv. Meanwhile, on the opposite end of the country, in Donetsk, a gang, which includes the current president of Ukraine, gathers for a meeting. Despite a severe frost, Yarko lives in a tent, like tens of thousands of rebels. Before the climax of this conflict, a Heavenly Hundred of peaceful, unarmed protesters will have given their lives for the Revolution and thousands of others would suffer in their defense of freedom and the independence of Ukraine. The citizens of the Free World will feel as if they are at the brink of a bloody Armageddon when they hold this requiem book in their hands.

Vasyl Baziv is a prominent Ukrainian political scientist, former diplomat and academic. He was one of the organizers of the National Democratic movement in 1989-1990, a professor at the "Ukraine" International University and holds the highest Ukrainian Diplomatic rank possible, having been appointed an ambassador. He is a member of the National Union of Writers of Ukraine and the author of many books, including a collection of essays in four volumes, *The Path from Slavery*, and also the two book *The Saga of Humanity's Cosmic Destiny: the End of the World and After*.

The Saint of Santa Fe ($20, ISBN: 978-1-937536-56-5, $35: Hardcover ISBN: 978-1-68114-141-1, LCCN: 2013956964, 198pp, 6X9", April 2014): In 1968, a young, recently ordained Colombian priest leaves behind everything to start a new parish in the jungles of Panama. Father Héctor Gallego soon discovers that his parishioners live as indentured servants. Inspired by liberation theology, he sets into motion a plan to liberate them. Father Gallegos is successful, but his work places him on a collision course with General Omar Torrijos, the nation's absolute ruler. On January 9, 1971, military operatives abduct the priest. He is never seen or heard from again, but he remains very much alive in the minds of Panamanians who, still today, clamor for his case to be brought to justice. Although The Saint of Santa Fe is a work of fiction, the novel is based on the real-life experiences of Héctor Gallego and the campesinos who worked alongside him to create a just society. *The Saint of Santa Fe* is a story of faith, heroism, and sacrifice that's reminiscent of Graham Greene's The Power and the Glory and Miguel de Unamuno's San Manuel Bueno, mártir.

Silvio Sirias is the author of *Bernardo and the Virgin* (2005) and *Meet Me under the Ceiba* (2009), winner of the Chicano/ Latino Literary Prize for Best Novel. In 2010, Silvio was named one of the "Top Ten New Latino Authors to Watch (and Read)." He has a doctorate in Spanish from University of Arizona. He also published academic books on Julia Alvarez, Rudolfo Anaya, and Salomon de la Selva. He has a collection of essays titled *Love Made Visible: Reflections on Writing, Teaching, and Other Distractions.* The Routledge Companion to Latino/a Literature lists him among the handful of authors who are introducing Central American themes into the U.S. Website: www.silviosirias.com.

Poetry

Battle for Athens ($15, ISBN: 978-1-937536-31-2, $30: Hardback ISBN: 978-1-68114-162-6, LCCN: 2012912824, 6X9", 56pp, July 2012): "What we left behind is not always what we return to. 'Battle for Athens' is a collection of poetry from Anna Faktorovich, who uses her poetry to tell the story of World War II veterans returning to Athens, Tennessee, to a city run by a corrupt government. Telling of the veterans rising up politically, then arming themselves violently, 'Battle for Athens' is a riveting twist of poetry with an enticing premise, much recommended…" –James A. Cox, Editor-in-Chief, *Small Press Bookwatch:* December 2012, *Midwest Book Review*

ANNA FAKTOROVICH is the Director and Founder of the Anaphora Literary Press. Previously, she taught college English for three years at the Edinboro University of Pennsylvania and the Middle Georgia State College. She has a Ph.D. in English Literature and Criticism. She published two academic books with McFarland: *Rebellion as Genre in the Novels of Scott, Dickens and Stevenson* (2013) and *The Formulas of Popular Fiction: Elements of Fantasy, Science Fiction, Romance, Religious and Mystery Novels.* She published two poetry collections *Improvisational Arguments* (Fomite Press, 2011) and *Battle for Athens* (Anaphora, 2012). She published two fantasy novellas with Grim's Labyrinth Publishing including, *The Great Love of Queen Margaret, the Vampire* (2014). She won the MLA Bibliography, Kentucky Historical Society and Brown University Military Collection fellowships.

The Third of Seven: ($20, 274pp, 6X9", ISBN-13: 978-1-68114-230-2, LCCN: 2016900719, Edited by Cortney Radocaj; January 2016): Suffering from short-term amnesia, Abram Jacobson wakes up in a new dimension without the slightest idea of how to get home. Joining forces with a dazzlingly attractive but deceptively strong native, Abram journeys to breathtaking new lands, encounters strange lifeforms, and constantly struggles to survive. But his troubles only start with him being trapped in a new dimension, and he soon learns an evil lord intends to murder everyone from back home. Abram is forced to fight for his life and the lives of his entire dimension, but after a while, he discovers that no one can be trusted. He realizes that if he ever wants to see the familiar sights of home again, he must overcome his limitations and fulfill a destiny that he knows stretches beyond his abilities.

JEREMIE GUY graduated from Towson University with an English degree and a creative writing minor. He has written and edited freelance for a number of organizations, and he sometimes dabbles as a ghostwriter for fiction and nonfiction. He has won first place in a handful of writing contests, and his creative works have appeared in a variety publications, including an appearance in Earthbound Fiction's short story anthology *Dark Stars.* He is a member of Lambda Iota Tau, international literary honors society.

Virgin Queen ($15, 92pp, 6X9", ISBN: 978-1-937536-98-5, $30: Hardcover ISBN: 978-1-68114-117-6, LCCN: 2014919876, December 2014): is a portrait of Queen Elizabeth I. Focusing on her interior life, it traverses her tragic love affairs and her fraught relationship with Mary, Queen of Scots, the cousin she never met. These pages illustrate her moments of defeat, her defiance, her strategies, her secrets, and her deathbed scene.

"Catherine Corman gives us an admirable companion in prose poems and photographs to one of England's greatest monarchs." —Lord Patten of Barnes, Chancellor of The University of Oxford

CATHERINE CORMAN'S work has been exhibited in the Venice and Berlin Biennales. Her book of photographs, *Daylight Noir*, is in the collection of The Museum of Modern Art Library. She is the editor of *Joseph Cornell's Dreams*.

Romanticism: ($15, 112pp, 6X9»), Print ISBN: 978-1-68114-213-5, EBook ISBN: 978-1-68114-214-2, LCCN: 2015916705; November 2015): is a collection of collage poems made from the memoirs, letters and diaries of Martha Graham, Anaïs Nin, Marguerite Duras, Billie Holiday and Diane Arbus. Photographs trace their paths through cafes, hotels, bars and museums of the cities in which their lives played out: Paris, London and New York. "Romanticism," wrote Anaïs Nin, "was an obsession with the far in place of the near… the unattainable in place of the attainable."

"Catherine Corman has recast the words of these five bold women into vital, independent poems, and in so doing, she has given their voices new energy and a new, personal clarity. These verses, by turns wistful, severe, wry, generous, bitter, resolute, and compassionate, are, alongside Corman's luminous photographs, a pleasure to read." —Lydia Davis

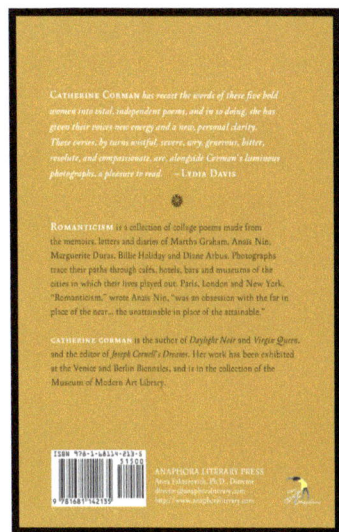

Meditation on Woman: Poems ($15, ISBN: 978-1-937536-13-8, $30: Hardcover ISBN: 978-1-68114-176-3, LCCN: 2011945635, 6X9", 80pp, December 2011): "Deceptively quiet, these meditations are ferocious, deep, cathartic—pouring light on the dark places of the human condition while extracting humor out of the little ironies of daily life. *Meditation on Woman* is a beautiful book that will prove a sturdy companion for those who are prepared to dig below the surface." —David Cole, Publisher, Bay Tree Publishing

"Aline Soules' new book, *Meditation on Women*, explores women's realities, dreams, and imaginary worlds. Her fifty-six eloquent prose poems are sometimes humorous, sometimes poignant, and always creative. Treat yourself to this collection." —B. Lynn Goodwin, Managing Editor, *Writer Advice*, http://www.writeradvice.com; *You Want Me to Do What? Journaling for Caregivers* (Tate Publishing, 2008)

ALINE SOULES' poetry and short fiction has appeared in journals, e-zines, and anthologies such as *100 Words, Literature of the Expanding Frontier*, and *Variations on the Ordinary. The Size of the World* was co-published with *The Shape of the Heart* by Plain View Press. Poems from *Evening Sun* appeared in *Kaleidowhirl, Reed, Shaking Like a Mountain, Houston Literary Review*, et al. Prose poems from *Meditation on Woman* appeared in *Tattoo Highway, Poetry Midwest, Long Story Short, Kenyon Review*, et al. Visit her blog at http://alinesoules.wordpress.com.

Birds on Elephant ($15, 6X9", 70pp, ISBN: 978-1-68114-002-5, $30: Hardcover ISBN: 978-1-68114-111-4, LCCN: 2014959352, January 2015): all of the landscape is an allusion, and "we borrow or skim on [it], and our work becomes more fertile." Each poem in the collection either perches on a great work or a famed poet, or has first words that make a sentence if read downward—as in:

Across and Down

Frame your memory so I could see it tomorrow.
Your place in mine has gone off with the tide.
Memory is not quite the warmth that was once on me.
So gather the particles and weigh in; it's not too dispersed.
I will look up and fly the gossamer of you yesterday.
Could you withstand the mind without the frame?
See it against the sea.
It will elevate with the sun. I'll just diminish
tomorrow.

TED BERNAL GUEVARA divides his eagerness, his out-of-bed thrill, into two compartments: Fiction, a rustic room where things are arranged and accessible with a calendar tacked on the wall above his head, and Poetry, the balcony attached to that room. He hardly urges himself to stand up and walk out. He just does, and the air out there is profoundly fresh. Guevara is the author of *Films*, a book of 55 poems based on 55 movies, and three novels, *A Circle with Two Corners, Days of Slint*, and *True Feel*. He resides in Speedway, Indiana.

THIS MORTAL EARTH
A Year of Beginnings and Ceasings

Fred Waage

This Mortal Earth: A Year of Beginnings and Ceasings: ($15, 114pp, 6X9", ISBN: 978-1-68114-008-7, $30: Hardcover ISBN: 978-1-68114-109-1, LCCN: 2015930077, January 2015): The poems in this collection were written one-a-day, during the course of the author's sixty-seventh year. They seek to express an ecological awareness, the "intense consciousness of land" (Aldo Leopold), a consciousness of the Earth's land and of that essence that composes the writer's being.

FRED WAAGE is Professor of Literature and Language at East Tennessee State University. He was raised in upstate New York, got his academic degrees from Princeton, and taught in many U.S. states including California, Illinois, and Pennsylvania. He has had many nonacademic jobs including Research Associate at the Huntington Library and Assistant Manager at Jack-in-the-Box. He also published chapbooks, poetry, and fiction. His most recent book is *Sinking Creek Journal: An Environmental Book of Days.*

Invisible Mending: Poems: ($15, 134pp, 6X9", Print ISBN: 978-1-68114-009-4, EBook ISBN: 978-1-68114-011-7, Hardcover ISBN: 978-1-68114-108-4, LCCN: 2015901604, March 2015): A themed poetry collection—a kind of "séance"—an evening to get in touch with other *souls,* and the world they once lived in. Yet, as a linked collection, the poems trace the arc of a life from birth to death, from childhood to old age, and move towards a spiritual journey in art. Our lives seem to be vanishing acts, perfected from birth to death. The collection suggests that the "real horror" is losing a loved one. But, while the poems keep an eye on death, the point is *life,* even the contemplation of a life beyond death. Certainly, there is remembrance—a time to mend our wounds—both visible and invisible. *Invisible Mending* tries to connect with the joy and grief that binds us all.

The Blessing of the Bikes & Other Life-Cycles: Poems: ($15, 112pp, 6X9", ISBN: 978-1-68114-092-6, Hardcover ISBN: 978-1-68114-106-0, April 2015): a themed collection in three parts that catalogues and values urban life. It chronicles the way we imagine and re-imagine the city. In so doing, the poems become urban praise songs. What would we miss if it were all to go missing? These poems measure the value of our neighbourhoods and the spirit of the city that we wish to preserve.

ANTHONY LABRIOLA'S work has appeared in *The Canadian Forum, PRISM international, Lo Straniero, Vallum: New International Poetics, Stone Voices,* and *Still Point Arts Quarterly, Passion: Poetry.* He studied at the University of Toronto and holds an M.A. in Drama. He taught English, Drama, and Performing Arts for thirty-two years. His other poetry collections include: *The Rigged Universe* (Shanti Arts) and *Sun Dogs* (Battered Suitcase Press). Anaphora Literary Press has published his prose works: D*evouring the Artist, The Pros & Cons of Dragon-Slaying*, and *Poor Love & Other Stories.* He teaches at Seneca College.

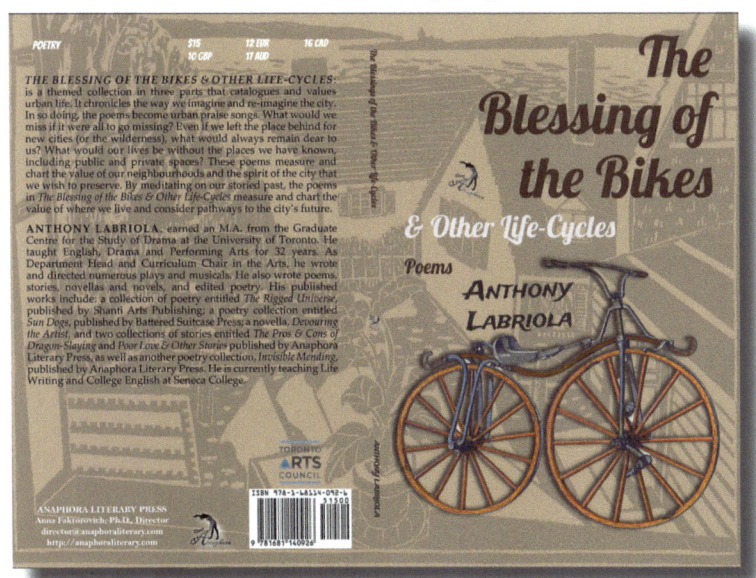

Inversed: ($15, ISBN: 978-1-937536-62-6, $30: Hardcover ISBN: 978-1-68114-138-1, LCCN: 2014933259, 6X9", 92pp, February 2014): In these poems, Jason Holt explores unusual word patterns that can help thoughts and feelings break free from the structures of habit and convention. Word-work and play come together here—in an attempt to resolve, by expressing them, the inevitable conflicts of raw experience.

Jason Holt lives in Wolfville, Nova Scotia and teaches at Acadia University. He received his Ph.D. in philosophy from Western University in 1998. His books include *Blindsight and the Nature of Consciousness*, which was shortlisted for the 2005 CPA Book Prize. *Inversed* is his sixth book of poetry.

"A new book by the inimitable Canadian poet Jason Holt always offers an adventure both exhilarating and terrifying. The reader will delight to find his trademarks of condensed diction and spare syntax, scintillating settings for his huge subjects in powerfully implosive poems that have consistently set Holt apart from all the other poets of his generation. But the poems of *Inversed* burn even brighter with the cold fire of Holt's word-passion, fluttering like a titanium butterfly on a pica." —Liane Heller, *Exposures* and *Code of Silence*

Behind the Steel: One Life—Five Epochs: ($15, 96pp, 6X9", ISBN: 978-1-68114-005-6, $30: Hardcover ISBN: 978-1-68114-113-8, LCCN: 2014922633, December 2014): takes the reader on a journey through Twentieth Century America, its cities, its wars, the western prairies, and the poet's encounter with death, losses of the heart, and old age, when the past stands still and time quickens, when the echoes of the past ricochet and scatter into pure energy. The poet sharply searches for meaning through action, but discovers that only in solitude does he find answers, albeit conditional, bowing to the forces beyond his sensibilities, to the limits of a self-imposed blindness, to the incomprehensibly complicated and absurd events that occur in our midst, yet exceed the human capacity for reason, moral belief and even suffering.

Joe Carvalko's poetry has appeared in journals, e-zines, and anthologies such as *Manifest West* (University Press of Colorado), *The Flagler Review*, *Anomalie Magazine*, Missouri Humanities Council and Missouri State University Press, *Military Writers Society of America Anthology, Military Experience and the Arts*, and other publications. His recent novel, *We Were Beautiful Once, Chapters from the Cold War*, (Sunbury Press, 2013), was judged a finalist for Best Historical Fiction, (Military Writers Society of America, 2014). He recently authored *The Techno-human Shell: A Jump in the Evolutionary Gap*, about how future medical technology will transform us into part cyborg. Other publications include: *A Road Once Traveled, Life from All Sides*, a narrative on the fabric of American life, *A Deadly Fog*, a collection of poems, essays, and short stories about war in America, and *Science and Technology a Guidebook for Lawyers* (ABA, 2014), as well as numerous articles on law, science and technology. He holds degrees in writing, law and engineering.

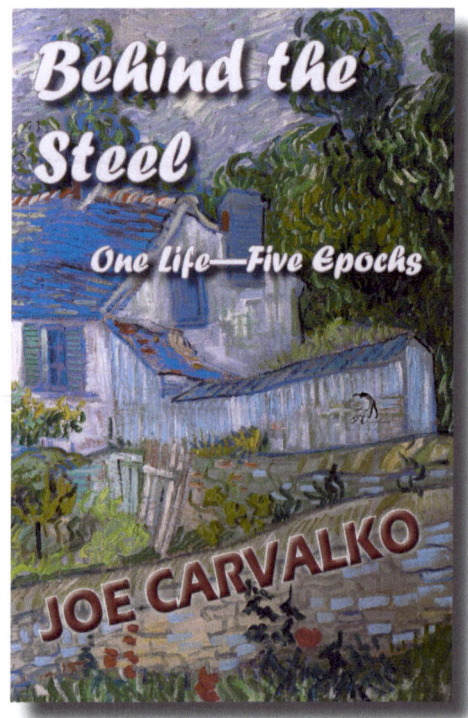

Voices Against Silence: ($15, ISBN: 978-1-937536-86-2, $30: Hardcover ISBN: 978-1-68114-124-4, 6X9", 98pp): employs a variety of tones, ranging from the deadly serious to the humorous, as, celebrating language, it addresses materials drawn from both the human and natural worlds. In accordance with this, it stands ready, at one moment, to contemplate a pet cat, at another, the cosmos.

ALAN HOLDER was born and bred in Brooklyn, and then received his A.B., M.A. and Ph.D from Columbia University. Over a period of forty years he taught at Columbia College, University of Vermont, University of Southern California, Williams, and Cornell, but principally at Hunter College of the City University of New York. He has published four books and several articles in the field of literary criticism. For two years after retiring, he wrote a weekly column on the environment for *The Redding Pilot*. He also served as a teacher's assistant in day-care centers. Having specialized in the teaching of poetry during his career, he continues to teach it at The Ridgefield Public Library. His poems have appeared in a variety of venues, and he is the author of two chapbooks of verse, *Opened: A Mourning Sequence* and *Aging Heard in the Clouds.*

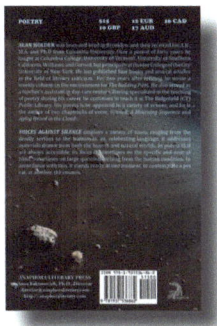

Sky Gazer: ($20, 142pp, 6X9", Print ISBN: 978-1-68114-207-4, EBook ISBN: 978-1-68114-208-1, LCCN: 2015915803, April 2016): Firmly rejecting the unabashed subjectivity and accompanying impenetrability of much contemporary verse , Alan Holder's *Sky Gazer*, from first to last, makes its poems steadily available to the reader, assumed to be "a creature of feeling" and addressed directly. The reader is onboard for a train ride or in-step for a woodland walk. It continually registers that great commonality of human experience, the four seasons. The poems share the sights that come the poet's way—so much of what he sees assumes the status of spectacle—the source of many of those arresting sights being the heavens, which Holder never tires of contemplating. He has a fondness for long, winding verse sentences; some poems consist of but a single one. Again and again, Holder alludes, sometimes implicitly, to works by great figures of the literary past—Shakespeare, Milton, Wordsworth, Tennyson, Melville, Twain, Yeats, Frost, Stevens, Eliot, Dylan Thomas—using them as springboards to go his own way. Repeatedly, his poems raise questions that do not admit of answers. *Sky Gazer* takes seriously one of the prescriptions for poetry that Stevens sets forth in Notes toward a *Supreme Fiction:* "It Must Give Pleasure."

"Whether addressing vegetarianism, the natural world, or the experience of jogging, Holder's poems are invitations to enjoy, think, and discuss. This accessible collection of poems, replete with cultural references, is an excellent choice for poetry workshops for teens and a stimulating choice for book-talks." —Hilary Crew, February 2015, *VOYA Magazine*

Skewed: A Collection of Poems: ($20, 6X9", 232pp, ISBN: 978-1-937536-95-4, $35: Hardcover ISBN: 978-1-68114-118-3, LCCN: 2014919151, October 2014): Beware—these poems are skewed, in other words, they deviate from the straight line. Enter a world of betting with God, hard-boiled detectives, the rigors of Pundit School, drinking at the VFW, the joys of divorce, Russian brides, Jesus' cell phone, bull riders, cartoon doctors, first world worries, grammar hospitals, drinking with clowns, and the worries of a clown. This book will shift your brain out of normal-mode, and will teach it the joys of taking the odd turns. Become *Skewed*.

PHILIP THEIBERT: holds an MFA in Writing and has worked as a speechwriter, copywriter, reporter, editor, and technical writer. His most recent books include: *Collisions at Home: The Baseball Poems of Philip Theibert*, *The Blockbuster Book of Brain Expanding, Creativity Enhancing Writing Exercises*, *Potato Chip Economics* and *The Most Creative, Escape the Ordinary, Excel at Public Speaking Ever*. Additional books written include: *Business Writing for Busy People*, *How To Give A Damn Good Speech*, *Lessons in Corporate Change*. Theibert's articles have been published in *The Wall Street Journal*, *Writer's Digest*, *Toast Masters*, *Executive Speaker*, *Vital Speeches*, *Manager's Journal* and other publications. Short stories and poems have appeared in *Mobius*, *AURA*, *The Steel Toe Literary Review*, *Wingspans*, *Capstone*, *The Scribe* and other publications. Theibert is a Pushcart Prize nominee.

Because There Was No Sea: ($15, 86pp, 6X9", ISBN: 978-1-937536-96-1, $30: Hardcover ISBN: 978-1-68114-119-0, LCCN: 2014955728, November 2014): "combines a mastery of simile with a Blake-like ability to build whole worlds from a grain of sand (or a phone, which 'may as well be a conch/from off the beach'). This is a restless, Janus-faced collection, simultaneously looking back on childhood memories of Bermuda ('alive, fresh as raw meat') and thirstily drinking in the details of the wider world." –Jacob Silkstone, editor of *The Missing Slate*

"Nancy Anne Miller's poems embrace island icons with a ruthless tenderness, teasing out their secrets and accepting with equal enthusiasm their surface beauty and their burdened hearts. Miller approaches the island's difficult colonial history from a position of exile and with a wondrous ability to find and restore the paradisiacal as she explores the mysteries of one place through the lens of the other." –Kim Aubrey, author of *What We Hold in Our Hands*

"Like hand-cut stones strung along a necklace, each of Miller's poems is its own gem. Untethered by theme, each page is a new discovery: a childhood memory, a lusty evocation of the landscape, an observation of passersby. We journey into these experiences finding fresh perspectives on our Island home." –Lisa Howie, Director of Bermuda National Gallery

NANCY ANNE MILLER, a Bermudian poet, has two poetry collections forthcoming: *Somersault* (Guernica Editons), and *Immigrant's Autumn* (Aldrich Press). She is a MacDowell Fellow published in *Edinburgh Review*, *Agenda*, *Magma*, *New Welsh Review*, *Interlitz: The International Literary Quarterly*, *The Fiddlehead*, *The Dalhousie Review*, *The Moth*, *Poetry Salzburg Review* and *Journal of Postcolonial Writing*.

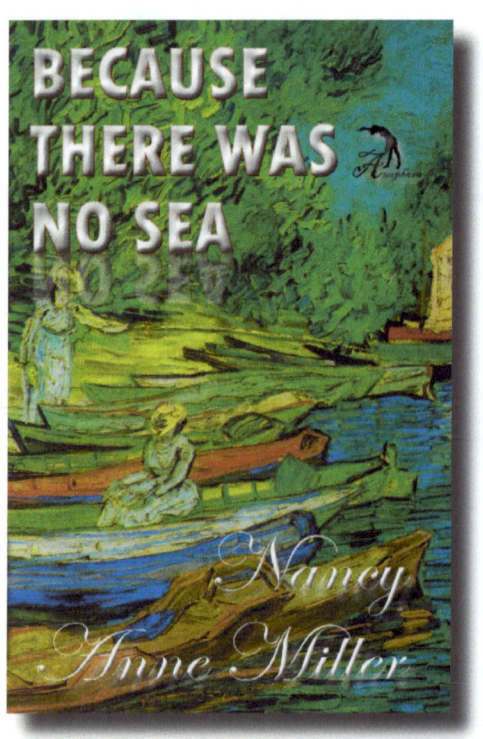

Compartments: Poems on Nature, Femininity and Other Realms ($15, ISBN: 978-1-937536-00-8, $30: Hardcover ISBN: 978-1-68114-184-8, LCCN: 2011912611, 6X9", 146pp, July 2011): "Carol Smallwood blends history and nature with the personal and domestic in powerful poems that are both current and timeless."—Kate Hopper, *Use Your Words: A Writing Guide for Mothers*; editor, Literary Mama

"Sifting my way through a pile of poetry submissions to English Journal several years ago, I came to Carol Small-wood's work. To say that her poems both pleased me and gave me pause is an understatement. Here were poems, most of them quite short, that were at once tight, vivid, subtle, and quietly profound, poems about what seemed to be nothing much but which spoke strongly of all manner of living things and of human beings making the best of a world we all want to understand more fully but that, in the long run, may be just out of our mental grasp."—James Brewbaker, professor, Columbus State University; poetry editor of *English Journal* (2003-2008)

CAROL SMALLWOOD is in *Best New Writing 2010*. She edited *Writing and Publishing: The Librarian's Handbook*, American Library Association, 2010. She's a National Federation of State Poetry Societies Winner, a Franklin-Christoph Poetry Contest Winner. The co-edited, *Women and Poetry: Tips on Writing*, *Women Writing on Family: Tips on Writing, Teaching and Publishing*: The Key Publishing House Inc., 2011 is her most recent anthology. Some of the Marquis publications Carol appears in are: *Who's Who in the World*, *Who's Who of American Women*.

The River Bends in Time ($15, ISBN: 978-1-937536-23-7, $30: Hardback ISBN: 978-1-68114-167-1, LCCN: 2012933922, PS3613.A975 R58 2012, 6X9, 110pp, April 2012): follows the flow of time and the river as it unwinds in a small town in Pennsylvania along the banks of the Susquehanna. The narrator experiences those quiet moments of joy when ducks come from the sky to skim the water's edge or in the height of a Nor'easter as he walks through the forest filling with snow, but also the sadness of a neighbor's dying or love breaking apart. The river flows, always bending and changing, like discovering the love of a mate that one joins with, becoming partners who run together under flying snow geese or dig a pond behind a two hundred year old house. Yet, the postmodern world seems lost without a past. A bout with colon cancer brings a renewed sense of the preciousness of each day and how the culture is wrong in its headlong race towards the future. The book ends with moments that resonate with the past in a state of continual affirming discovery.

GLEN A. MAZIS teaches philosophy and humanities at Penn State Harrisburg where he is Full Professor and has directed the interdisciplinary Master's program. His poetry has been published in several literary journals, including *Rosebud*, *The North American Review*, *Sou'wester*, *Spoon River Poetry Review*, *Willow Review*, *The Atlanta Review* and *Ashville Poetry Review* (best of 1994-2004). He also writes books of cultural critique and philosophy, including *Earthbodies* (SUNY, 2002) and his newest book, *Humans, Animals, Machines: Blurring Boundaries* (SUNY, 2008). Mazis's poetic credits include being a chapbook finalist for White Eagle Coffee Store Press, and a finalist in competitions for a Writers At Work Fellowship, and the White Pine Press and Spire Press Book Prizes.

Glurk! A Hellbender Odyssey: ($20, 160pp, 6X9", ISBN-13: 978-1-68114-231-9, 22 photographs, January 2016): is the first book-length, epic poem about *Cryptobranchus alleganiensis*, aka North America's largest salamander. Through an investigative poetic lens of folklore, history, science and ecology, grotesque-advocate Mark Spitzer paints a four-part profile of an amazing phenomenon. This semi-monstrous mosaic of a living, breathing barometer of water quality and biodiversity is accomplished through a visionary voice that incorporates research, data, primary sources, and images that twist and torque like an actual bender (as the mythology goes) wending its way back to hell.

MARK SPITZER is the author of twenty-three books, including fish books, novels, memoirs, collections of poetry, and literary translation. He is currently an associate professor of creative writing at the University of Central Arkansas, and the Editor in Chief of the award-winning literary journal, *Toad Suck Review* (toadsuckreview.org). For more information on Spitzer, take a look at sptzr.net.

"The poems range from scientific narratives to neologism-filled lyrics, connecting us to our own wildness, playing on our own youthful enthusiasms, humor and curiosity. Most importantly, the poet suggests that imagination begins the solution to even the most serious problem, even the threat of extinction." —Lea Graham, author of *This End of the World: Notes to Robert Kroetsch* (Apt. 9 Press, 2016)

"Mark Spitzer really captured the hellbender story here in an informative and entertaining manner. The presentation is digestible (not technical) and creative... This is a great way to reach a broad audience and convey the plight of this amphibian." —Dr. Donald Shepard, Amphibian Biologist, University of Louisiana, Monroe

Handful of Sand and Other Poems: ($15, 92pp, 6X9", Print ISBN: 978-1-68114-219-7, EBook ISBN: 978-1-68114-220-3, LCCN: 2015916951, October 2015): is a collection of images and feelings that linger in the conscience and refuse to go away. They evoke emotions the author is compelled to share with the reader in understandable language, without obscurity—plainly, deliberately. Whether it's observing an ant, watching a rocker sway to the breeze, or simply taking a train to the city, these poems help to grasp a deeper meaning in seemingly routine actions and incidents. Many insist we evolve from profound life-altering events that lay their mark on us. However, it's the unpretentious, simple occurrences throughout the years that shape who we are; it's the unimpressive handful of sand we overlook that holds a million lives.

STEVEN P. STAMATIS was born in Greece but grew up in Chicago during the 1960s. The cultural transition to American life set the stage for a lifelong love affair with the English language. Following a 35-year business career, he is now an instructor at Westwood College with a focus on English and Humanities. Steven has been writing poems for about 40 years and has been published in a dozen anthologies earning him a 1st place award in the Religion category. In addition, he has written three screenplays and two novels. Currently, he resides with his wife in Addison, Illinois.

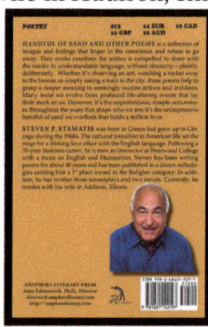

Skating in Concord ($15, 6X9", 82pp, ISBN: 978-1-937536-80-0, $30: Hardcover ISBN: 978-1-68114-131-2, LCCN: 2014946379, July 2014): These poems take readers into the world of Henry David Thoreau and his circle of acquaintances: Ralph Waldo Emerson, Margaret Fuller, Louisa May Alcott. These poems also bring Thoreau into the present, imagining him as a living entity in our lives—and with him comes a renewed appreciation for the beauty of the world around us, a world in which astonishment animates every moment. To read these poems is to be "nose-deep in life, too busy for the leaving of it."

JEAN LeBLANC grew up in central Massachusetts and still connects her love for nature and literature to the landscape and history of New England. She now lives and teaches in northwestern New Jersey, returning to her native place via poetry. Her collections include *The Haiku Aesthetic: Short Form Poetry as a Study in Craft* (Cyberwit.net, 2013) and *At Any Moment* (Backwaters Press, 2010).

Mathematics of Love (Soft cover $15, Hard cover $30, ISBNS: 978-1-937536-01-5, 978-1-937536-08-4, LCCN: 2011939734, 6X9", 134pp, October 2011): "Like his mentor Jose Garcia Villa, John Edwin Cowen is a brave poet. He takes poetic risks with language and the result is often a beautiful flower behind the barbed wire of craftsmanship. I love the variety of poems in *Mathematics of Love* and the charged-up voice that powers all the work. He can be tender, challenging, energetic, and as complex musically as Villa and his other love, Dylan Thomas. I recommend this book to all those who care about poetry and who care about the human spirit." —Peter Thabit Jones, Welsh poet, Founder and Editor of THE SEVENTH QUARRY— Swansea Poetry Magazine

"Concise, witty, subtle, these works move on the page with the ease of seasoned dancers on the stage. Cowen has a distinct taste for the lyrical, with a poetic lineage that includes Jose Garcia Villa, E. E. Cummings, Gerard Manley Hopkins, Dylan Thomas, and Emily Dickinson. And his language is as alive as it is exacting. The poems in *Mathematics* will leave you, as the poet declares in one, 'feeling / closely lobbied / by a / widened soul.' Amen!" —Luis H. Francia, Author, *Museum of Absences*

JOHN EDWIN COWEN is the *Parnasus Literary Journal's* first prize winner in international competition. He has published poems widely in major literary magazines and is former co-publisher of *Bravo: The Poet's Magazine* founded in 1980 by the late poet, Jose Garcia Villa. He is editor of the Penguin Classics centennial volume: *Doveglion: The Collected Poems of Jose Garcia Villa* published in 2008. Cowen is Professor of Literacy and Education at Fairleigh Dickinson University; he earned his doctorate at Columbia University.

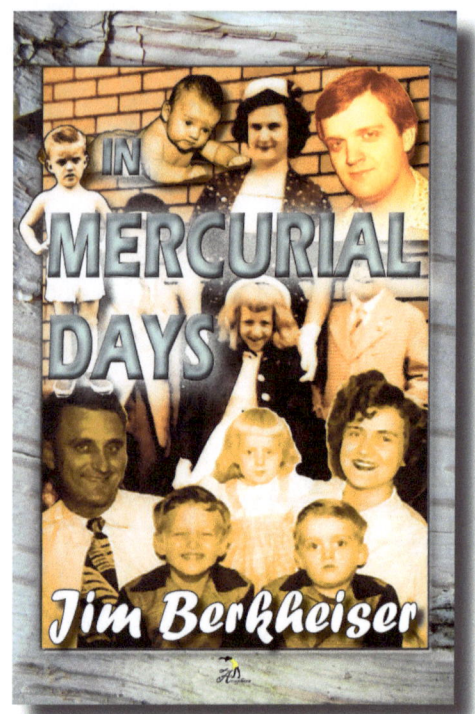

In Mercurial Days: ($15, 6X9", 104pp, Paperback ISBN: 978-1-68114-097-1, $30: Hardcover ISBN: 978-1-68114-103-9; $2.99: EBook ISBN: 978-1-68114-098-8, LCCN: 2015907959, June 2015): "'You wouldn't know anyone,' Jim Berkheiser writes in his poem 'Slide Show,' but of course we know everyone in the earnest, down-to-earth evocations of family and friends that comprise *In Mercurial Days*. From childhood games to adult farewells, the poems in this collection take us on a journey that is instantly recognizable. With a poet's sense of paradox, Jim Berkheiser offers us images that are at once individual and shared." — Jean LeBlanc, *Skating in Concord*

JIM BERKHEISER currently lives, works and writes in Sussex County, New Jersey, though he is a native Pennsylvanian and a graduate of Bloomsburg University. He is on the Advisory board for Betty June Silconas Poetry Center at Sussex County Community College and was Director of the Writers' Round Table, a group that encourages and promotes local writers, for eight years. Jim also has participated in the local Teen Arts Festival critiquing creative writing and poetry. Jim's poems have appeared in the *Paterson Literary Review*, *The Stillwater Review*, *Exit 13 Magazine*, and the *Journal of New Jersey Poets*. He received an Honorable Mention for the 2011 New Jersey Poets Prize and was nominated for the Pushcart Prize in 2010. When he is not working or writing, he is active in the local theater community as an actor.

Medusa's Hairdresser: Skyclad: ($15, 94pp, 6X9", Print ISBN: 978-1-68114-099-5, $30: Hardcover ISBN: 978-1-68114-186-2, $2.99: EBook ISBN: 978-1-68114-100-8, LCCN: 2015943201, June 2015): "is Bob Dylan's Blond on Blond converted to magnificent poetry. It will revolutionize poetry in a way that that album revolutionized music." —Klaus Gerken, poet and editor of *Ygdrasil Literary Journal*

"With all the cheek of a blasting cap, Maria Jacketti's poems unspring like a nest of hair." —Craig Czury, *Thumb Notes Almanac*

"Maria Jacketti's new release paints where the wind tells her to go. You will find no clichés in her work. From this book, one discovers an unprecedented journey into a world of surprising images. Make sure you don't read too long! You might find yourself cast in stone, forever lost in her language. A great book sure to entertain, enchant and stimulate a whole new approach to reading and appreciating poetry. Revolutionary work." —Melanie Simms, former Perry County Poet Laureate, President, Association of Pennsylvania Poets Laureate

"Showcases the beauty of her poetry, love of nature, family and the world, while also raging against that which is unjust and unfair." —Regina Drasher, Northeastern Pennsylvanian performing artist and writer

MARIA JACKETTI is the poet laureate of Hazleton, Pennsylvania and a reporter and columnist at The Hazleton Standard Speaker. She holds an M.A. in creative writing from New York University and has received a poetry fellowship from the Pennsylvania Council on the Arts. Her book-length translations of Pablo Neruda and Gabriela Mistral have been read worldwide for more than two decades.

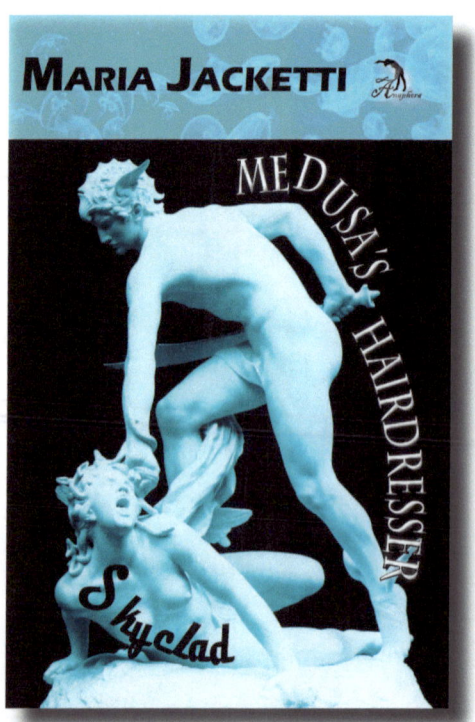

Seven: ($15, 6X9", 60pp, Print ISBN: 978-1-68114-095-7, $2.99: EBook ISBN: 978-1-68114-096-4, $30: Hardcover ISBN: 978-1-68114-104-6, LCCN: 2015941134, May 2015): "Antonio Hopson spins gentle legends and quiet love stories. From biker goddesses to mythical tricksters, from feuding winds to debauched taverns, the subjects of 'The Vernal Equinox of Death and Kisses and Other Short Stories' reveal the author's romantic enchantment with the world around him, even when it's at its grittiest." —Dru Pagliassotti, Editor, *The Harrow*

"Antonio Hopson writes with a subtle power and a minimalist's sense of economical prose. His affecting style comes on slowly and dances beneath the surface, evoking abstract emotions that stretch beyond the short boundaries of his flash-fiction. Layered and dense, his writing belongs to the prose genre but employs the artistic precision of poetry." —Mike Dell'Aquila, Editor, *Farmhouse*

"Antonio Hopson writes with the sense and instincts of a Jack Keruoac, combined with the cultural eye for detail of a Chuck Klosterman. All five senses thrive when reading his prose, which moves through you like the Snoqualmie River itself." —Jon Horowitz, *The Wonder Boy Review*

ANTONIO **J. H**OPSON**'S** work has appeared in *The Harrow*, *SNReview*, *Ascent Aspirations*, *Lost Magazine*, *The Piker Press*, Akashic Books' *Mondays Are Murder* series, and NPR commentator Andrei Codrescu's *Exquisite Corpse*. He received Farmhouse Magazine's Reader's Choice Award and was invited to perform at Seattle's Richard Hugo House as a featured writer. He was selected to participate in Evergreen College's Literary Conference on "Activism and the Avant-Garde" and is a national EPPIE Award finalist.

The Island of Charles Foster Kane ($15, ISBN: 978-1-937536-45-9, $30: Hardback ISBN: 978-1-68114-152-7, LCCN: 2013936553, 6X9", 98pp, March 2013): If some of the more pleasant productions of our civilization were to be crated up for a long desert island sojourn, one might just as well choose to pack along Oprah Winfrey as Wallace Stevens, or place lyrical tributes to the eccentric reggae artist Dr. Alimantado alongside those to Bob Dylan or Tom Waits. One might wish to include notes on superheroes and celebrities, sound bites, search strings, and assorted tweets and puns. The poetry and experimental fiction in M. V. Montgomery's new collection *The Island of Charles Foster Kane* not only cover a wide range of literary possibilities, but offer an entertaining reflection of the world all around us.

M. V. MONTGOMERY is an English and film professor at Life University in Atlanta. He is the author of three previous poetry collections: *Joshu Holds a Press Conference*, *What We Did With Old Moons*, and *Strange Conveyances*, which Muscle & Blood Magazine named best poetry book of 2010. His creative work has appeared in over a hundred literary journals and e-zines in a dozen countries and has been nominated for Best of the Net, Pushcart, and PEN/Faulkner awards.

Elvis Presley's Hips & Mick Jagger's Lips ($15, ISBN: 978-1-937536-36-7, $30: Hardback ISBN: 978-1-68114-157-2, LCCN: 2012955068, April 2013, 7 illustrations, 6X9", 80pp): is rock and roll in poetry. The poems cover a range of subjects related to music, organized into three sections: "The Honey Thing," (relationships); "Mood Alteration," (substance abuse and shifts in emotion); and "Write a Song About It," (the music business and its relationship to other aspects of life). Each poem also departs in unique ways from rock and roll, its lyrics and history.

Susana **H. C**ase, a professor at the New York Institute of Technology, has published *The Scottish Café* (Slapering Hol Press), *Anthropologist In Ohio* (Main Street Rag Publishing Company), *The Cost Of Heat* (Pecan Grove Press), *Manual of Practical Sexual Advice* (Kattywompus Press), and *Salem In* Séance (WordTech Editions). Please visit her online at: http://iris.nyit.edu/~shcase/.

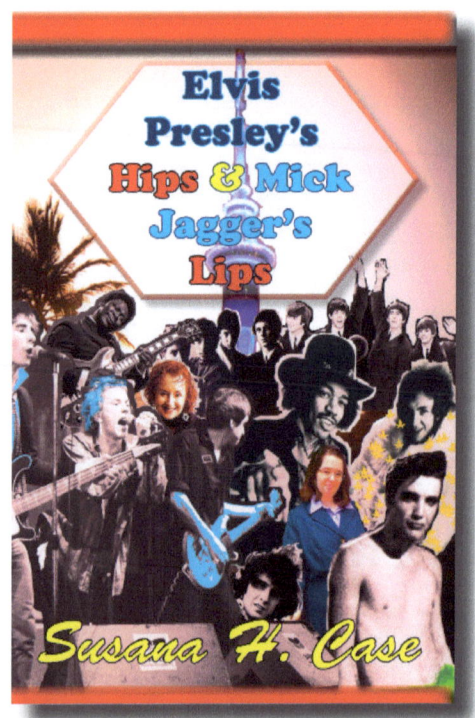

Earth and Below ($15, August 2013, 9X6", 112pp, 42 illustrations, Poetry, ISBN: 978-1-937536-48-0, $30: Hardback ISBN: 978-1-68114-149-7, LCCN: 2013946740, 2013) is an illustrated story, in a sense, everything one ever wanted to know about copper, examining the labor issues involved in the history of attempts to organize copper workers, their working conditions, the way differing outlooks, most commonly class-based, but not exclusively so, impacted upon the lives of copper workers, and copper and copper mines as objects in a larger world.

This is a harrowing, intense book. It carries on the great work and vision of Muriel Rukeyser's Book of the Dead on a global scale. Poet and sociologist Susana H. Case has written a deeply moving "elegy of loss" and a sustained indictment of the copper mining industry from Chile to Calumet, Rhodesia to Boston. Her prose poems and selection of photographs give voice to human suffering in unforgettable ways, as if etched in acid on a copper plate. It takes courage just to read this book. —Anthony DiMatteo

At a time when the fundamental rights of workers are in peril, Susana H. Case's unflinching Earth and Below investigates the rarely seen lives of those who mine the earth at great personal risk and compels us to look anew at the goods "unearthed" from their work. Although Case employs a wide range of voices, time periods, and locales, her focus is on the individual, the family, and the community navigating the brutal challenges of the mining companies and on the earth itself. The overall effect is both panoramic and yet always intimate. Graced throughout by striking archival photographs, this extraordinary excavation into the world beneath is at once timely and timeless. —Yermiyahu Ahron Taub

Queen of the Platform ($15, ISBN: 978-1-937536-54-1, $30: Hardcover ISBN: 978-1-68114-145-9, LCCN: 2013956258, 84pp, 6X9", December 2013): These poems are based on the life of Laura Madeline Wiseman's great-great-great-grandmother, the nineteenth century lecturer, suffragist, and poet, Matilda Fletcher Wiseman (1842-1909) and the men in her life: her brother, George W. Felts (1843-1921), a civil war solider who was later charged with murder, her first husband, John A. Fletcher (1837-1875), a school teacher and a lawyer, and her second husband, William Albert Wiseman (1850-1911), a minister who became her agent. Like her seven brothers who served in the Civil War, Matilda chose the public sphere. After the death of her only child, Matilda joined the lecture circuit. She spoke to support herself and her first husband, until his death. On the stage she spoke among other lecturers of her time, such as Susan B. Anthony.

Laura Madeline Wiseman's *Queen of the Platform* is not only full of the energy of immediacy, but also deep meditation on the material traces of her ancestry. Sometimes exacting, sometimes provocative, but always bold—Wiseman's poetry sharply observes the fabric of her characters' lives. —Margo Taft Stever, author of *Frozen Spring*

LAURA MADELINE WISEMAN: A Lecturer at the University of Nebraska, Lincoln, with a PhD in English, and numerous publications in poetry (*Unclose the Door, Sprung,* and *Farm Hands*), women's studies (*Women Write Resistance: Poets Resis Gender Violence*), and other areas. She has also won several awards including the Academy of American Poets Award, the Susan Atefat Peckham Fellowship, and many others.

Light's Battered Edge: Poems: ($15, 96pp, 6X9", Print ISBN: 978-1-68114-217-3, EBook ISBN: 978-1-68114-218-0, LCCN: 2015917029, November 2015): "Catches sight of 'a sparrow by its own forgotten self,' and that sparrow stands in for other 'forgotten' ones: the homeless, the wrecked, the ill, a family of forebears 'visited' by comprehensive Job-like 'Misery.' These compelling poems leave us disquieted, as much by beauty as by sorrow." —Nathalie F. Anderson, Professor, Swarthmore College

"Think of the spirit of place as the frame of memory shaping language, of the perpetual soliloquy of being who you are in counterpoint with echoing phrases others have uttered at or to you, and you will have some idea of the chant and enchantment of the poems gathered in Light's Battered Edge. There are some hard truths in these poems—about abusive spouses, about the wear and tear of caring for others. But underlying it all is the sense of what love really means." —Frank Wilson, *Books, Inq.; The Epilogue*

"She is now making her mark as a poet." –Justine Heinze, *Roxborough-Manayunk Patch*

DIANE SAHMS-GUARNIERI is the author of two full-length poetry collections: *Images of Being* (Stone Garden Publishing) and *Night Sweat* (Red Dashboard Press). She has been published in *The Philadelphia Inquirer, Pennsylvania Literary Journal, Many Mountains Moving, Philadelphia Stories, Blue Collar Review,* and *Wilderness House Literary Review,* among others. Awarded a grant in poetry from the AEV Foundation in 2013, she is the 2015 "Winner" of Partisan Press's "Working People's Poetry Competition." She currently serves as Poet in Residence at Ryerss Museum and Library and as Poetry Editor of the Fox Chase Review. More info about Guarnieri: dianesahms-guarnieri.com

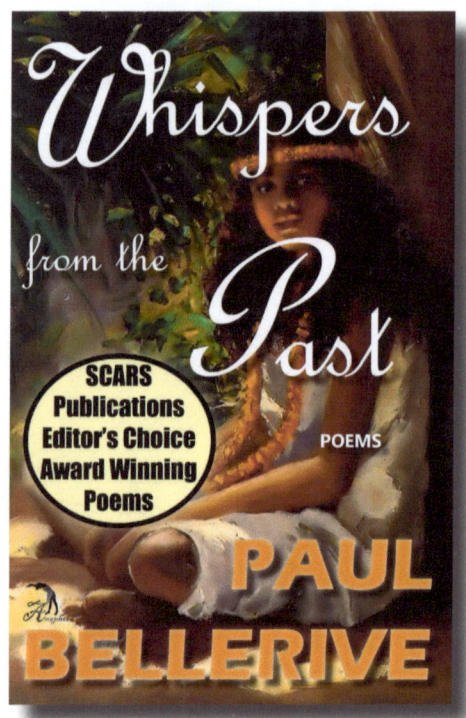

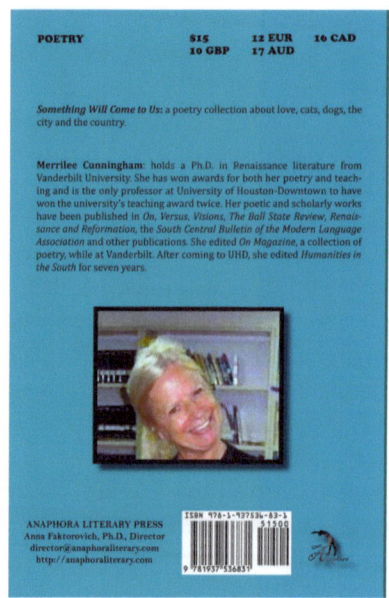

Whispers from the Past: Poems: ($15, 116pp, Print ISBN-13: 978-1-68114-187-9, ISBN-10: 1681141876, EBook ISBN-13: 978-1-68114-188-6, Hardcover ISBN-13: 978-1-68114-189-3, LCCN: 2015910908, 6X9", July 2015): An old teacher's attempt to sound a warning (or perhaps a lament) that as a society we are in danger of losing touch with our history, our literary traditions, and our cultural heritage. In this his fifth book and third poetry collection, the award-winning poet, Paul Bellerive attempts to rediscover and then to capture the artistic bits that combined with our personal experiences are the DNA of who and what we are.

PAUL BELLERIVE has been writing and teaching writing at the college level for more than thirty years. His fiction and poetry have appeared in numerous anthologies, magazines, reviews, and journals. *Whispers from the Past* is his fifth book. His work has received two PushCart Prize nominations, and won the SCARS Publications Editor's Choice Award for poetry in 2013 and 2014. He is also a recipient of the Bay Area Poets Coalition (Berkeley, California) Award for Excellence.

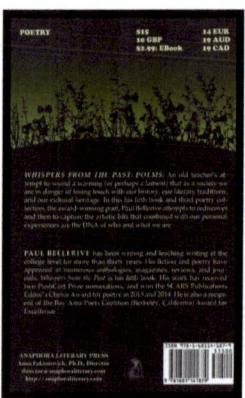

Something Will Come to Us ($15, ISBN: 978-1-937536-83-1, $30: Hardcover ISBN: 978-1-68114-129-9, LCCN: 2014949808, 6X9", 94pp, September 2014): a poetry collection about love, cats, dogs, the city and the country.

MERRILEE CUNNINGHAM: holds a Ph.D. in Renaissance literature from Vanderbilt University. She has won awards for both her poetry and teaching and is the only professor at University of Houston-Downtown to have won the university's teaching award twice. Her poetic and scholarly works have been published in *On, Versus, Visions, The Ball State Review, Renaissance and Reformation,* the *South Central Bulletin of the Modern Language Association* and other publications. She edited *On Magazine,* a collection of poetry, while at Vanderbilt. After coming to UHD, she edited *Humanities in the South* for seven years.

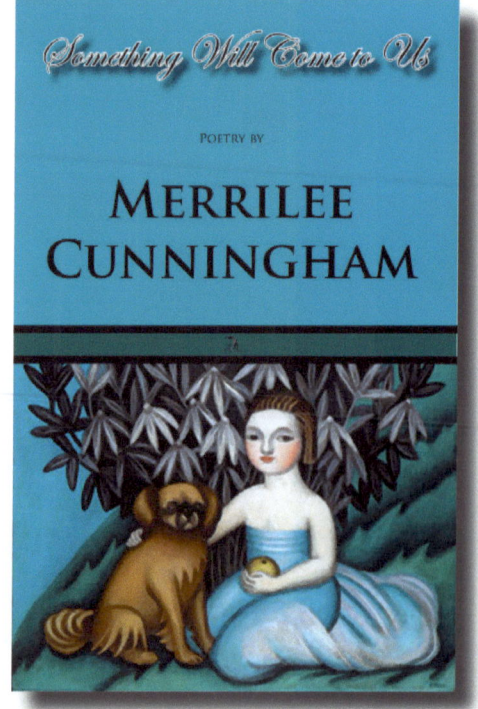

Mind and Body: And Other Stories: ($20, 130pp, 6X9", ISBN-13: 978-1-68114-233-3, February 2016): is a subtly linked series of stories that chronicle two generations of a family from the Depression to World War II to the Vietnam War to the present. Characters include a jazz trumpeter, a Ukrainian teenager taken by the Nazis for slave labor in Germany, soldiers from World War II and the Vietnam War, and a strange crew of college professors and their wives from a small college in the Midwest.

Lucas Carpenter was born in Elberton, Georgia. He was educated at the College of Charleston (B.S.), the University of North Carolina at Chapel Hill (M.A.), and the State University of New York at Stony Brook (Ph.D.). He is the author of *John Gould Fletcher and Southern Modernism* (U. of Arkansas Press, 1990) and general editor of a seven-volume series devoted to Fletcher's work. He has also written a chapbook of poetry, *A Year for the Spider* (UNC Pitcher Poetry Award, 1973), and a book of poetry, *Perils of the Affect* (Mellen Press, 2002). His poems, stories, articles and reviews have appeared in thirty-seven periodicals, including *Prairie Schooner*, *The Minnesota Review*, *Beloit Poetry Journal*, *College Literature*, *Kansas Quarterly*, *Carolina Quarterly*, *Concerning Poetry*, *Poetry* (Australia), *Southern Humanities Review*, *College English*, *San Francisco Review of Books*, *Callaloo*, *Chronicle of Higher Education*, and *New York Newsday*. He was awarded a Fulbright fellowship to lecture and write in Belgium during the 1999-2000 academic year. He is Charles Howard Candler Professor of English at Oxford College, Emory University.

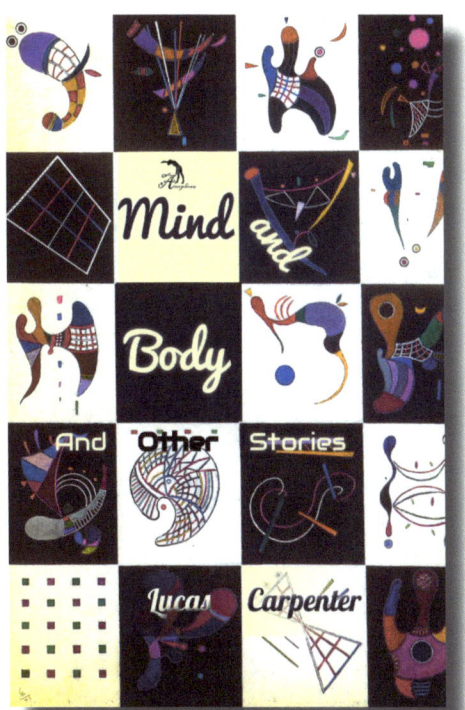

Blood and Gypsies: ($15, 78pp, 6X9", ISBN-13: 978-1-68114-235-7, February 2016): In this two-part study of a dysfunctional Italian, New York family and the dream-like series of vignettes, Lenny DellaRocca blends the hard-nosed with the atmospheric. In one world, he is a character in his own lower class, uneducated cast of sisters, brothers, parents, aunts and uncles, and in the other, an observer of fragmentary, dark and sometimes sinister stories set in imaginary towns and landscapes.

Lenny DellaRocca's work has appeared in *Poet Lore*, *Poetrybay*, *Albatross*, *2River view*, *Fairy Tale Review* and *Nimrod*. His chapbook, *The Sleep Talker*, is available from Night Ballet Press. DellaRocca was instrumental in bringing to South Florida such poets as Denise Duhamel, Albert Goldbarth, Yusef Komunyakka, Carolyn Wright and Lyn Lishin. A Pushcart nominee, his Electric Chair Poetry Reading was a sought-after South Florida event, which featured handpicked poetry readings. DellaRocca works for a blood center and lives in Delray Beach, Florida with his wife, Marie Herrera.

Children's Books

Dragonflies in the Cowburbs ($15, 6X9", 104pp, ISBN: 978-1-937536-51-0, $30: Hardcover ISBN: 978-1-68114-146-6, LCCN: 2013917417, September 2013): "poignant, witty, and lyrical vignettes formally reminiscent of *The House on Mango Street*. This coming-of-age narrative captures so much of our contemporary zeitgeist, from Facebook status updates to a bad case of 'textitis.' She has found a way to sing with grace and conviction." —Julie Marie Wade, *Wishbone: A Memoir in Fractures* and *Small Fires: Essays*

"A charming glimmer of hope for the future, a world in which today's young people are able to do more than merely cope as they strive to make sense of a world that most often appears to be without harmony, logic, or compassion." —A.M. Garner, *Undeniable Truths*

DONELLE DREESE: author of two poetry chapbooks: *A Wild Turn* and *Looking for a Sunday Afternoon*. Her work has appeared in publications such as *Quiddity International*, *Hospital Drive*, *Roanoke Review*, *Connotations*, *Souvenir*, *Appalachian Heritage*, *Runes*, *Gulf Stream Magazine*, *Journal of Microliterature*, *Gadfly Online*, and *Conclave*. She was selected as a semi-finalist for the 2013 Louise Bogan Award for Artistic Merit and Excellence by Trio House Press. Donelle is also the author of *America's Natural Places: East and Northeast*, a work of travel writing. She is an Associate Professor of English at Northern Kentucky University.

The Sloth and I ($30, ISBN: 978-1-937536-29-9, LCCN: 2013904133, 32pp, 30 illustrations, 8.5X11", March 2013): A girl grows tired of her suburban life and runs away to the Amazon jungle, where she meets a group of talking sloths and enjoys some intense relaxation and lots of fun. Has she found a new home or will her home call to her? This is a great book for kids, one full of fantastic descriptions and original artwork.

ANNA FAKTOROVICH is an English professor, poet, illustrator and book publisher. She has traveled to Italy, Israel, Ukraine, China, Canada, and all over the U.S. in her search for amazing creatures and adventures.

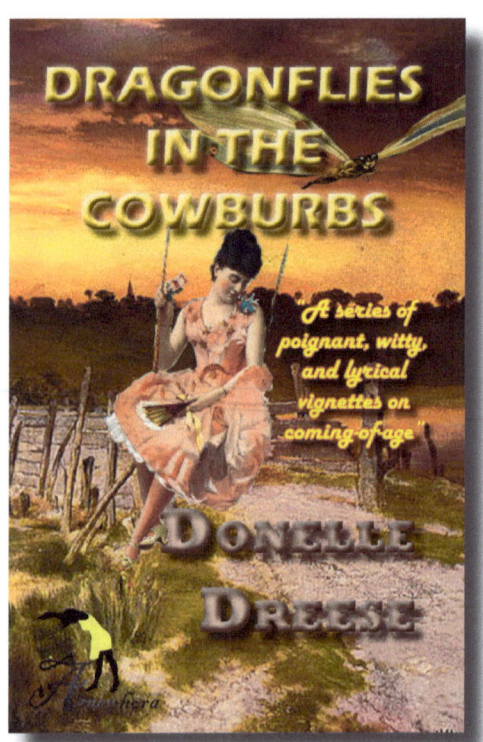

Short Stories

Dangerous Obsessions ($15, ISBN: 978-1-937536-16-9, $30: Hardcover ISBN: 978-1-68114-107-7, LCCN: 2011945742, PS3610.A735 H68 2011, 6X9", 106pp, January 28, 2012): 2015 Books of the Year! Short Fiction: "Of the dozen stand-out individual short story collections I enjoyed in 2015, Van Laerhoven's was the standy-outiest. [His] stories always surprise without descending into the cheap thrills of fakery and he uses his journalistic experience to write about the cold and the cruel aspects of human nature with unflinching truth." —Hubert O'Hearn, *San Diego Book Review*

"A philosophical exploration of the human condition, a confrontation with the darkest corners of our minds. I highly recommend this moving and gripping collection of stories to anyone seeking to be moved by something truly thought-provoking." —*Quick Book Reviews*, David Ben Efraim

"Recommend it to anyone who likes short, dramatic & down to the earth crime/mystery stories 4/4*" —*OnlineBookClub*

Bob Van Laerhoven: a fulltime Belgian/Flemish author, Laerhoven published more than 30 books in Holland, Belgium and the US. Three-time finalist of the Hercule Poirot Prize for best mystery novel of the year with the novels *Djinn* and *The Finger of God*. Winner of the Hercule Poirot Prize for *Baudelaire's Revenge*, which also won the USA Best Book Award 2014 in the category "mystery/suspense". His last novel, *De schaduw van de Mol* is currently being translated into English as *The Shadow of the Mole*.

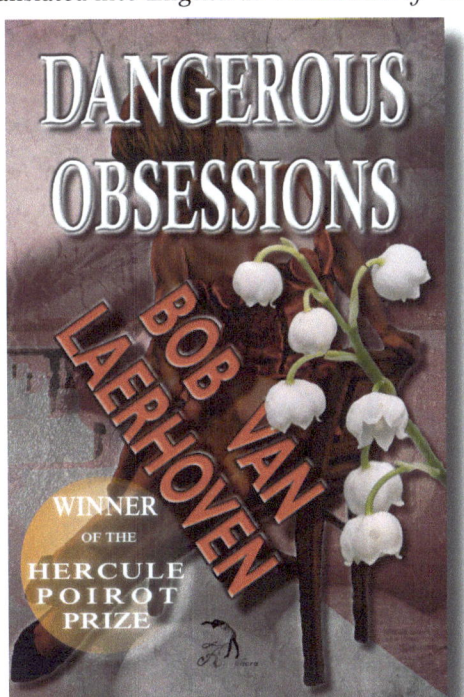

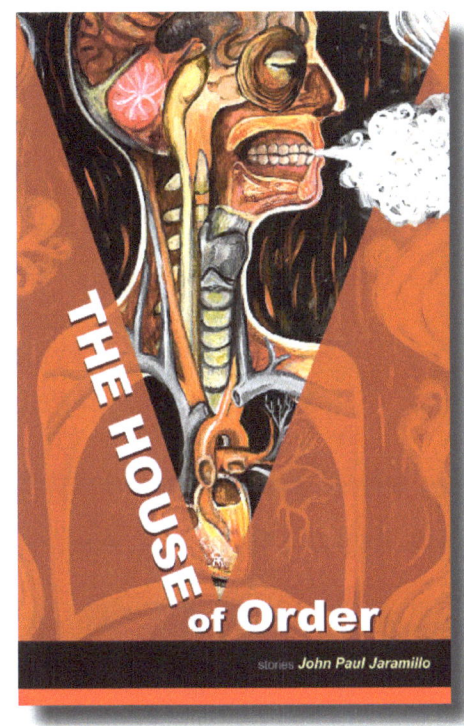

#6 on the 2013 Top 10 New Latino Authors to Watch (and Read) List

The House of Order ($15, ISBN: 978-1-937536-16-9, $30: Hardback ISBN: 978-1-68114-170-1, LCCN: 2011945742, PS3610.A735 H68 2011, 6X9", 106pp, January 2012): the first collection of composite stories by John Paul Jaramillo, presents a stark vision of American childhood and family. Set in Southern Colorado and Northern New Mexico, Manito's only access to his lost family's story is his uncle, the unreliable Neto Ortiz. Manito sorts family truth from legend as broken as the steel industry and the rusting vehicles that line Spruce Street.

"These stories find John Paul Jaramillo hitting his stride as an acute observer and chronicler of hard and valuable lives. The writing conveys great warmth and understanding. This is a career to watch." –Tracy Daugherty, author of *One Day the Wind Changed*

John Paul Jaramillo grew up in Southern Colorado but now lives, writes and teaches in Springfield, Illinois. He earned his MFA in creative writing (fiction) from Oregon State University and, currently, holds the position of Associate Professor of English in the Arts and Humanities Department of Lincoln Land Community College.

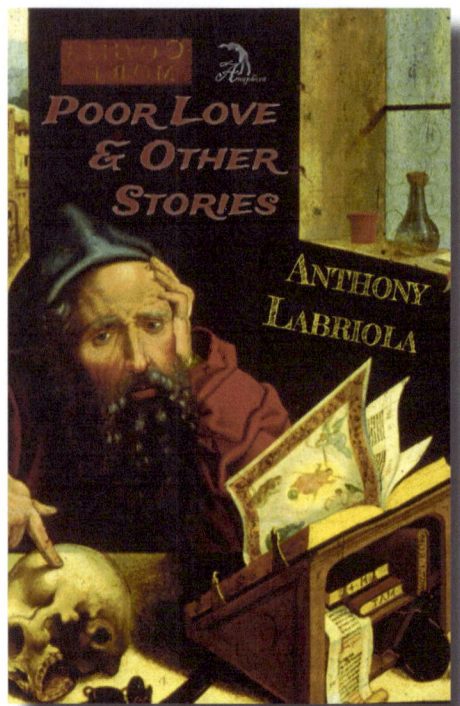

Poor Love & Other Stories ($20, 174pp, 6X9", ISBN: 978-1-68114-000-1, Hardcover ISBN: 978-1-68114-115-2, LCCN: 2014921796, December 2014): These stories, in all their narrative voicings, deal with sorrow and still seek to find life's joys. Despite conflicts, contradictions, sacrifices, surprises and ironies, the haunted and hunted characters try to *comprehend death in detail*. In so doing, the human spirit rises up and triumphs against the incomprehensible and bewildering aspects of life, love and death.

ANTHONY LABRIOLA is married to his childhood sweetheart, Louisa Josephine. They have five grown-up children—all of whom are artists in a variety of arts. Though he was born in Italy, he grew up in Canada. He studied at the University of Toronto and received a B.A. in English and French, a B.Ed. in English and Dramatic Arts, and an M.A. from the Graduate Centre for the Study of Drama. He taught English, Drama and Performing Arts for 32 years. Then went on to teach Life Writing at Seneca College in Toronto, Ontario. Some of his work has appeared in *The Canadian Forum*, *Prismin-ternational*, *Lo Staniero*, *Vallum Magazine*, *Stone Voices*, *Still Point* and *Passion: Poetry*. A collection of poetry, *The Rigged Universe*, published by Shanti Arts, is out now. Vagabondage Press is set to publish another poetry collection, *Sun Dogs*, in May, 2014.

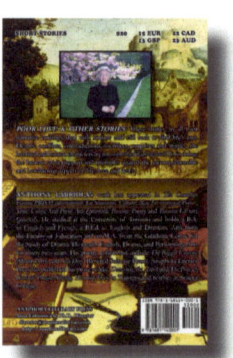

The Pros & Cons of Dragon-Slaying: Collected Stories: ($19, 338pp, 6X9", ISBN: 978-1-937536-65-7, Hardcover ISBN: 978-1-68114-135-0, LCCN: 2014937916, April 2014): This collection shows us the battles—fought, lost and won—when we strive to live life to the fullest. In the fabled adventures in both this world and the next, there are many quests to be embarked on, with countless clashes with dragons—seen and unseen. In *The Pros & Cons of Dragon-Slaying*, the characters struggle with the bewildering aspects of existence and try to prevail against the forces that are arrayed against them, or that are besieging them from within. Despite their multiple points of view, which range from the farce to the surreal, these *crusade* stories all speak in harmony, as they reveal life's stunning surprises and twisted ironies. The tales also speak for life against death, for love against apathy, and for the human spirit against all forms of oppression. But as you weigh the pros and cons of dragon-slaying, take care to watch out for the tempters and demons of inwardness.

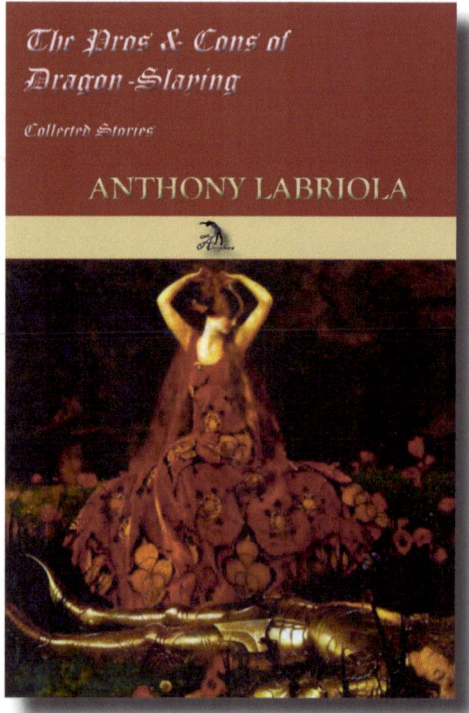

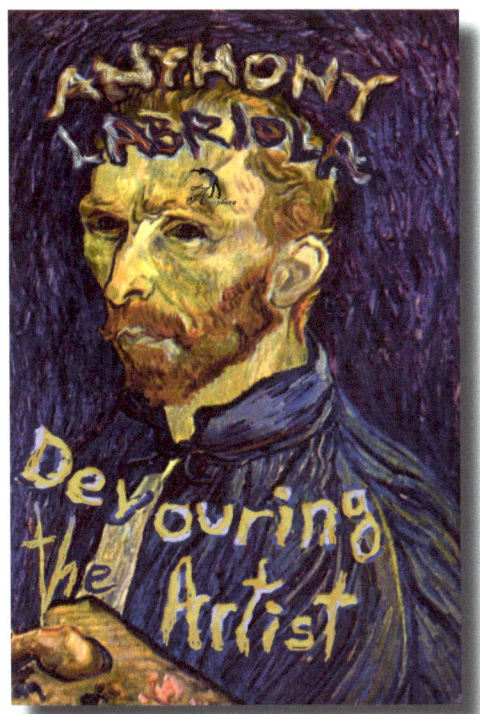

Devouring the Artist ($15, ISBN: 978-1-937536-63-3, Hardcover ISBN: 978-1-68114-137-4, LCCN: 2014935003, 6X9", 80pp, March 2014): Set in the late sixties and early seventies in Montreal and Paris, the novella deals with Sebastien Elia, a young but accomplished artist, and his anarchic relationship with Lee Archer, a Canadian-born student-artist. Sebastien introduces him to the violence of life, sex and art. His rapacious hunger to devour experience draws Lee and a small group of intimates into a world of free love, social, artistic and sexual experimentation and rebellion. The sexual revolution is in full swing, but so is political unrest. Lee begins a love affair with another art student, Anne Asher. Sebastien's betrayal of a student cell of the FLQ in Quebec makes him a marked man and the target for political revenge. On the run, he returns to Paris, pursued by agents on a dark mission to assassinate him. When one of Sebastien's "temporary muses" is murdered, Lee and Anne set out for Paris and are drawn into Sebastien's sexually charged dark world of hunger, love and revolt.

Spirit of Tabasco: ($15, ISBN: 978-1-937536-89-3, $30: Hardcover ISBN: 978-1-68114-126-8, LCCN: 2014951609, 110pp, 6X9", October 2014): is a glimpse at the mystifying experiences of people young and old, working through circumstances that ultimately change their worldly perspectives. The stories include the travails of a young man who volunteers to give care to a mute, conniving ex-con dying of tongue cancer, a cynic who attends a lecture on compassion and is held captive by an ominous fellow-pilgrim, a teenager who goes with his friend to steal back a rifle, only to have the friend aim the gun at him and then shoot himself (in the foot), and a young girl who is lured by her odd older cousin to go trick-or-treating in early July. The novella tells of a precocious teen who helps his mother retrieve a mysterious and possessed ancient Mayan mirror from the hands of his greedy estranged father.

RICHARD DIEDRICHS: grew up in Los Angeles. He edited travel and health magazines in Seattle, worked as an editor at the schools of engineering and public health at the University of California, Berkeley, and then taught Fourth and Fifth Grades, and Kindergarten, in public elementary schools around the San Francisco Bay Area. He has published short stories in literary journals and two novels, *Neither Coming Nor Going* and *Cherry Blossom.* He currently lives on the island of Hawaii.

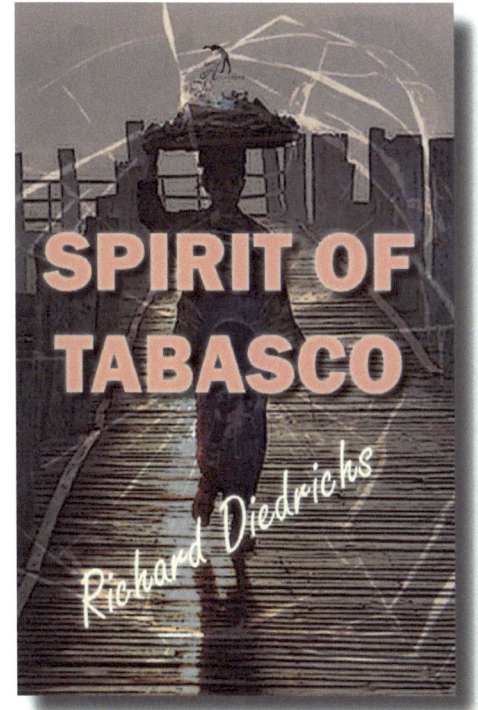

Pennsylvania Literary Journal

ISSN#: 2151-3066

EDITOR: ANNA FAKTOROVICH

Pennsylvania Literary Journal (Catalog #: PN80 .P46)is a printed peer-reviewed journal that publishes critical essays, book-reviews, short stories, interviews, photographs, art, and poetry. PLJ is available through the EBSCO Academic Complete and ProQuest databases in full-text. It is also on sale as single issues on Amazon, Barnes and Noble and most other online bookstores. It is listed in the MLA International Bibliography, the MLA Directory of Periodicals, Genamics JournalSeek, and Duotrope's Digest. The journal is a member of the Council of Literary Magazines and Presses. PLJ has published works by and interviews with established journal editors, Sundance Film Festival and Brooklyn Film Festival winners, and best-selling authors and scholars.

Interviews with Geraldine Brooks and Farmers: Volume VII, Issue 1: ($15, 166pp, 7X10", Spring 2015, 84 photographs, ISBN: 978-1-512068-34-4): This issue begins with an interview with the Pulitzer Prize winning author, Geraldine Brooks, who talks about the writing craft, her novels and her life outside of fiction. This feature is followed by four interviews with farmers from the Frankfort, Kentucky region, one of whom, Michael Spencer, is on the Kentucky state Farm Bureau board and another, Richard Jones, runs the regionally well-known Happy Jack's Pumpkin Farm. The critical essays include one from the editor, Anna Faktorovich, on the Kentucky farm cabin myth, which is best-recognized as the Lincoln cabin myth.

Interviews with Best-Selling Young Adult Writers: Volume IV, Issue 3 ($10, Fall 2012, ISBN-13: 978-1-937536-38-1, $30: Hardback ISBN: 978-1-68114-156-5, 6X9", 112pp): Interviews with Cinda Williams Chima, James Dashner and Carrie Ryan, all New York Times best-selling young adult fiction writers. They are interviewed by Catherine W. Griffin, who has a Master's of Science in Journalism from Columbia University. They share their experiences with writing in a popular genre, and give specific advice for both new and professional writers. Those who love reading their books should appreciate this close inside look into their minds and lives. You will also find Thomas Carlyle's 1840 2nd edition of Chartism and a couple of critical reviews of new academic books.

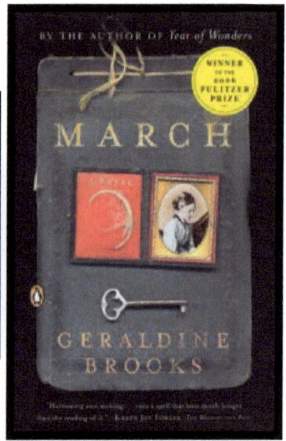

INTERVIEW WITH LARRY NIVEN: VOLUME V, ISSUE 2 ($10, 6X9", SUMMER 2013, 68PP, ISBN: 978-1-937536-49-7): This special issue of the Pennsylvania Literary Journal: Interview with Larry Niven features an interview with the best-selling science fiction author, Larry Niven, in which he discusses the writing craft, the life of a professional writer, and his unique science fiction style. Niven's Ringworld has won many prestigious international awards, and his newly released collection of short stories, The Draco Tavern is one of the best recent examples of structured, literary science fiction. The issue also includes a short story from the editor, Anna Faktorovich, "Coal and Rice" about a struggling Chinese rice farmer and a wealthy, corrupt Chinese businessman. Kehinde Wiley, a Yale MFA graduate's painting is on this issue's cover.

Interview with Mary Jo Putney: Volume VII, Issue 2: ($10, 6X9", 80pp, ISBN: 978-1-68114-196-1, 10 photographs, Summer 2015): Features an interview with Mary Jo Putney, a best-selling romance author. A ten-time finalist for the Romance Writers of America RITA, she won RITAs for Dancing on the Wind and The Rake and the Reformer and is on the RWA Honor Roll for bestselling authors. She has also been awarded two Romantic Times Career Achievement Awards, four NJRW Golden Leaf awards, and the Romance Writers of America Nora Roberts Lifetime Achievement Award. Also, an interview with an established poet and interim director of the Creative Writing Program at the University of Connecticut, Sean Frederick Forbes, interviewed by Rodrigo Rodriguez.

FILM THEORY AND MODERN ART: VOLUME VI, ISSUE 1 ($10, ISBN#: 978-1-937536-72-5, SPRING 2014, 6X9", 136pp): includes two interviews with the winners of the 2014 Sundance Film Festival, Nathan Zellner (*Kumiko, the Treasure Hunter*) and Janicza Bravo (*Gregory Go Boom*). It also features an essay from one of the most respected film academics in the world, Bert Cardullo, "Modish Artifice vs. Modern Art." There are also essays from Dr. R. Joseph Rodriguez, Dr. Keith Moser, and Aaron Lee Moore. You will also find innovative poetry from Jefferson Holdridge (the Director of the Wake Forest University Press), Louis Gallo (professor at Radford University), and Mark Jones (professor at Trinity Christian College). Finally, there is a review from the Editor, Anna Faktorovich, of a television series available in-full on Netflix, *Breaking Bad.* It is discussed at-length, with a focus on the elements that position it somewhere between great art and disastrous pop filmmaking, and a special look at acting methodology through a study of the supporting lead, Aaron Paul.

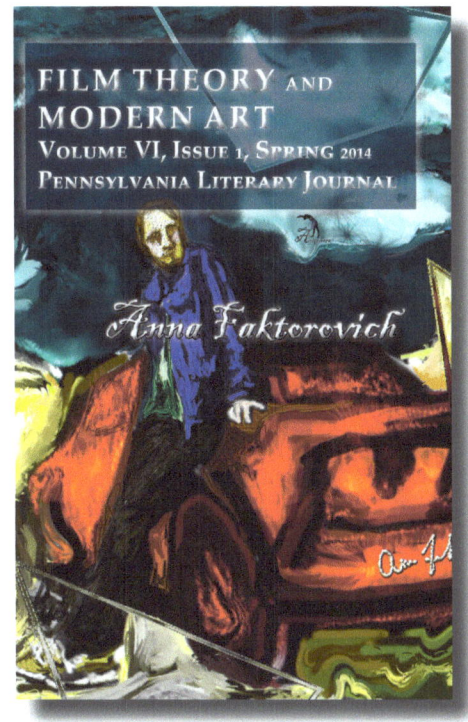

VOLUME IV, ISSUE 2: BROOKLYN FILM FESTIVAL INTERVIEWS, PART 2 ($10, ISBN: 978-1-937536-35-0, $30: Hardback ISBN: 978-1-68114-159-6, Summer 2012, 6X9", 116pp): One of the main sections is a new set of interviews with the winners of the Brooklyn Film Festival, and the second main section is two rebellious, anti-monarchical works from the 19th century by British authors. The Brooklyn Film Festival interviews with producer-directors focus on three films, none of which were made in New York. Dara Kell talks about making Dear Mandela, a film that focuses on the shanty town housing struggles in South Africa. Daniel Long discusses Pigeon Kicker, which looks inward at the psychology of a psychopathic youth. And Tina Gharavi explains her Indian film, I Am Nasrine, about the struggles of a woman in a chauvinist world. The rebellious stories are passionate, political statements that should be of interest to students of British political fiction and rhetoric. George Cruikshank, the infamous cartoonist and satirist presents his 1820 long, illustrated poem, The Queen's Matrimonial Ladder, which bitingly relates the various indescretions of the English Queen. In a later, 1838, unpublished essay, Jeremy Bentham makes the highly controversial at the time claim that like America, Canada should also be emancipated by the British Empire in Canada. Emancipate Your Colonies!

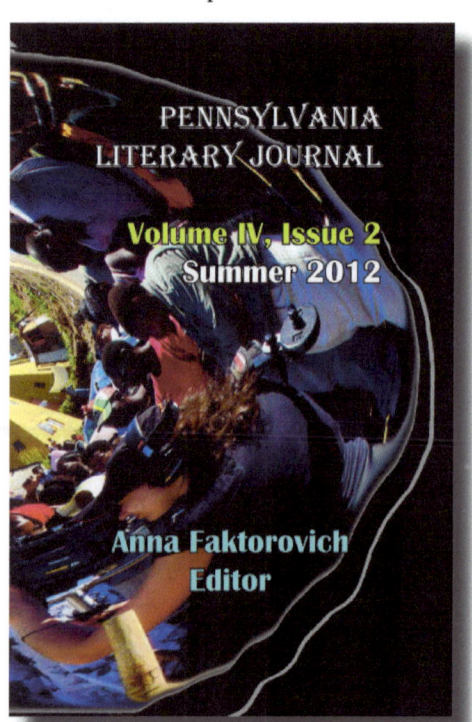

INTERVIEWS WITH BROOKLYN FILM FESTIVAL WINNERS: PENNSYLVANIA LITERARY JOURNAL: VOLUME III, ISSUE 2 ($40, ISBN: 978-1-937536-02-2, $40: Hardcover ISBN: 978-1-68114-183-1, SUMMER 2011, 6X9", 222pp): The Brooklyn Film Festival invites regional, national and international submissions. I conducted interview the directors, producers, script writers and other creative people, who won awards at the BFF in various categories. This issue should be very helpful for those who hope to build a film-making career. Antonio Piazza talks about transitioning from being a working Italian writer to creating a short film that has been shown in nearly 100 film festivals. Stephan Wassmann relates the dangers and adventures of filming bomb metal scrappers during war-time on the Mexican border. Ivaylo Getov describes how one can turn their senior NYU Tisch film school project into an award-winning venture. Massimiliano Verdesca covers special effects on a low-budget and techniques to use when working with actors. Yonah Lewis and Calvin Thomas chat about the frustrations of youth and the film industry in Canada. Damian Harper touches on the causes and ways to prevent gang-violence in Brooklyn and elsewhere. Joel Fendelman talks about theology and filming locations. Marina Mello boasts about filming in Brazil.

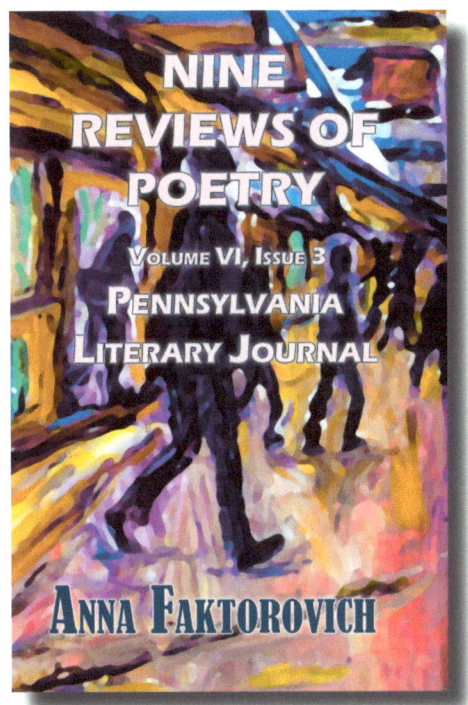

NINE REVIEWS OF POETRY: VOLUME VI, ISSUE 3: ($10, 148pp, 6X9", Fall 2014, ISBN: 978-1-68114-006-3): This issue includes nine reviews from the Editor, Anna Faktorovich, of recently released poetry collections, with a special look at the recurring styles and themes and cover design. The essays focus on modern and postmodern cultural artifacts. There are two essays on drama from a well-known film critic, Bert Cardullo. Michael Denison's essay is on the connections between the postmodern novel, *Gravity's Rainbow*, and the ancient Chinese game, Go. Keith Moser finds Foucauldian elements in a 2006 film, *Harkis*. You'll also find four short stories and poems from six poets.

Interviews with Gene Ambaum and Corban Addison: Volume VII, Issue 3, Fall 2015: ($20, 214pp, 6X9", ISBN: 978-1-519787-95-8, 40+ photographs): This issue includes an interview with Gene Ambaum, one of the creators of the popular *Unshelved* cartoon about a library. The second featured interview is with Corban Addison, the author of three international bestselling novels, *A Walk Across the Sun*, *The Garden of Burning Sand*, and *The Tears of Dark Water*. There is also the largest selection of extensive book reviews to appear in *PLJ* to-date with starred reviews in all genres, in fiction and non-fiction, and from both high and low-brow literature. The essays section includes Keith Moser's exploration of the post-Marxist philosophy of Jean Baudrillard and Michel Serres, and Marco R. S. Post's study of monologue and dialogue in J.M. Coetzee's Disgrace.

INTERVIEWS WITH NOVELISTS: VOLUME VI, ISSUE 2: ($10, 178pp, 6X9", Summer 2014, ISBN: 978-1-937536-84-8): Features interviews with best-selling and award winning novelists. Bob Van Laerhoven, winner of the 2007 Knack Hercule Poirot Prize, for his mystery novel, *Baudelaire's Revenge*, talks about his horses, literary fiction, and about the boundaries of obscenity. John Michael Cummings, winner of The Paterson Prize for Books for Young People for his novel, *The Night Freed John Brown*, discusses reasons for writing young adult fiction, selling the first novel to Penguin, and other curious topics. Bestselling visionary author of *The Transhumanist Wager*, Zoltan Istvan, chats about the adventures he had working for National Geographic, and the philosophy behind his unique novel. The issue also includes a review of *The Pizza Underground*, a comedy rock band of which Mack Culkin is a minor band member. The issue is illustrated with photographs from a New York City photographer, Jeremy Freedman. Fiction pieces include a short story from the Editor, Anna Faktorovich, "My Life as a Werewolf."

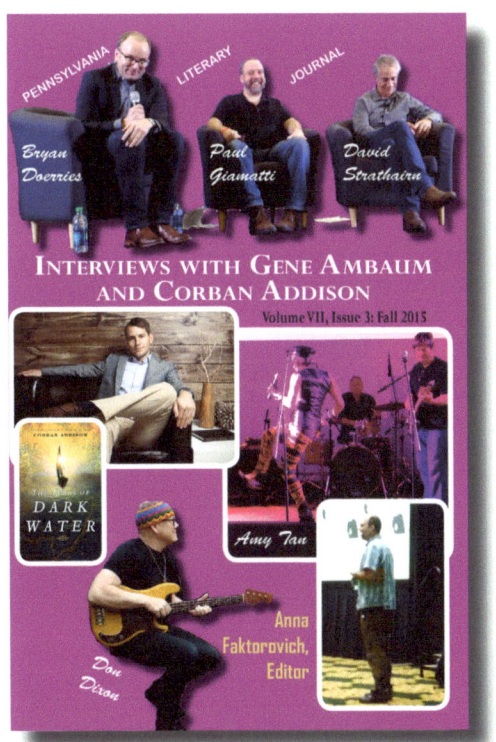

Other Titles

*Michael Connelly
A Reader's Guide*
Stan Schatt
$15, 150pp, 2012, HC/PB
ISBN: 978-1-937536-27-5

What Time Are You?
**Jeffry Atwood and
Charles A. Calio**
$15, 106pp, 2012, HC/PB
ISBN: 978-1-937536-28-2

Baby Pepper
Michelle Chen
$15, 52pp, 2012
ISBN: 978-1-937536-04-6

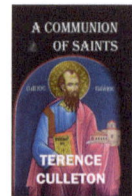

A Communion of Saints
Terence Culleton
$15, 2011, 76pp, HC/PB
ISBN: 978-1-937536-05-3

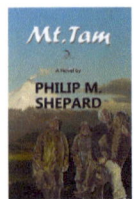

Mt. Tam
Philip Shepard
$25, 286pp, 2014, HC/PB
ISBN: 978-1-937536-59-6

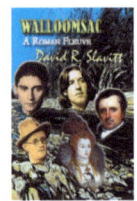

*Walloomsac:
A Roman Fleuve*
David Slavitt
$20, 176pp, 2014, PB/E
ISBN: 978-1-68114-026-1

Eyes of the Slain Woman
Benjamin Kwakye
$20, 2012
ISBN: 978-1-937536-20-6

Truths of the Heart
G. L. Rockey
$25, 2012, 332pp
ISBN: 978-1460983386

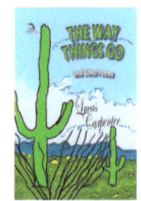

*The Way Things Go:
And Other Poems*
Lucas Carpenter
$15, 80pp, 2013, HC/PB
ISBN: 978-1-937536-42-8

Sky Sandwiches
John F. Buckley
$15, 98pp, 2012, HC/PB
ISBN: 978-1-937536-32-9

Nadia
Jack Lawrence Luzkow
$20, 270pp, 2012, HC/PB
ISBN: 978-1-937536-30-5

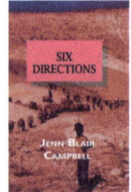

Six Directions
Jenn Blair Campbell
$15, 2011, 206pp, HC/PB
ISBN: 978-1-937536-03-9

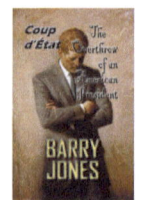

*Coup d'Etat:
The Overthrow of an
American President*
Barry Jones
$20, 126pp, 2014, HC/PB
ISBN: 978-1-937536-82-4

The Blue Maroon Murder
Gloria McMillan
$15, 202pp, 2011, HC/PB
ISBN: 978-1-937536-06-0

Rocks Full of Sky
Stephen Lefebure
$15, 88pp, 2013, HC/PB
ISBN: 978-1-937536-39-8

Rain, Rain, Go Away…
Mary Ann Hutchison:
$15, 132pp, 2011
ISBN: 978-1-937536-07-7

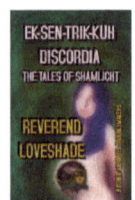

*Ek-sen-trik-kuh Discordia
The Tales of Shamlicht*
Reverend Loveshade
$15, 2011, 205pp, OOF
ISBN: 978-1-937536-18-3

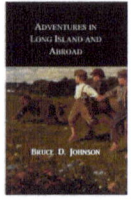

*Adventures in Long
Island and Abroad*
Bruce D. Johnson
$19.99, 2011, 348pp
ISBN: 978-1456549183

Under Centauri
Jeremy Gadd
$15, 96pp, 2013, HC/PB
ISBN: 978-1-937536-57-2

*Class of '67: Fancies,
Myths and Follies*
Paul Bellerive
$20, 148pp, HC/PB
ISBN: 978-1937536503

The Dandy Vigilante
Kevin Daley
$19, 252pp, 2014, HC/PB
ISBN: 978-1-937536-64-0

*PLJ: Reviews of Popular
Fiction: Volume V:1*
$10, 2013, 66pp
ISBN: 978-1-937536-46-6

PLJ: Volume V, Issue 3
Editor: Anna Faktorovich
$10, 2013, 160pp
ISBN: 978-1-937536-60-2

*PLJ: Creative Work
Volume III: Issue 3*
$10, Fall 2011, 68pp
ISBN: 978-1-937536-22-0

*British Literature
Volume 2, Issue 2*
$20, 2010, 208pp
ISBN: 978-1-456304-32-4

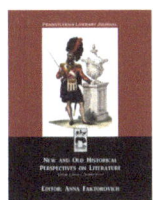
*New and Old Historical
Perspectives on
Literature: Vol. 2, Issue 1*
$15, 2010, 8.5X5.5", 272pp
ISBN: 978-1-450583-58-9

*PLJ: Editing Technique:
Vol. III, Issue 1*
**$10, 2011, 5.5X8.5", 114pp
ISBN: 978-1-461-16497-5**

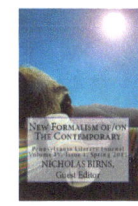
*New Formalism of/on the
Contemporary: Vol. IV:1*
$10, 6X9", 144pp
ISBN: 978-1937536244

Silence Imbibed
Jenn Gutiérrez
$15, 2011, 100pp
ISBN: 978-1-937536107

East of Los Angeles
John Brantingham
$15, 72pp
ISBN#: 978-1460925201

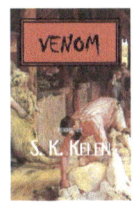
Venom
S. K. Kelen
$15, 90pp
ISBN: 978-1456566418

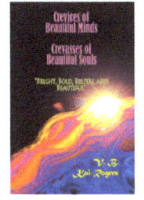
*Crevices of Beautiful
Minds*
V. B. Kai-Rogers
$15/$30, 120pp, 2012
ISBN: 978-1-937536-31-2

*Private Hercules
McGraw: Poems of the
American Civil War*
S. Thomas Summers
$15/$30, 86pp, 2012
ISBN: 978-1-68114-172-5

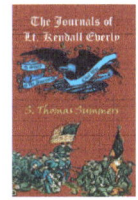
*The Journal of Lt. Kendall
Everly: A Story of the
American Civil War*
S. Thomas Summers
$15/ $30, 80pp, 2013
978-1-68114-151-0

*Death Is Not the Worst
Thing*
T. Anders Carson
$15, 92pp, HC/PB
ISBN#: 978-1463518127

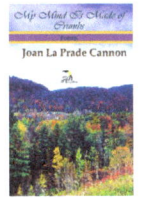
*My Mind Is Made of
Crumbs*
Joan La Prade Cannon
$15/$30, 100pp, 2013
ISBN: 978-1-68114-143-5

*Notes on the Road
to Now*
Paul Bellerive
$15/$30, 146pp, 2013
ISBN: 978-1-68114-150-3

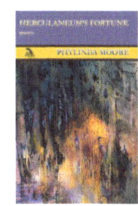
Herculaneum's Fortune
Phylinda Moore
$15/$30, 78pp, 6X9", 2014
ISBN: 978-1-68114-134-3

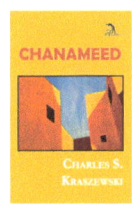
Chanameed
Charles S. Kraszewski
$15, 124pp, 2014, HC/PB
IBSN: 978-1-503289-11-6

Liberation from Tyranny
Ronni Kove
$15/$30, 2014, 84pp
ISBN: 978-1-68114-128-2

*Folk Concert:
Changing Times*
Janet Ruth Heller
$15/$30, 90pp, 2012
ISBN: 978-1-68114-165-7

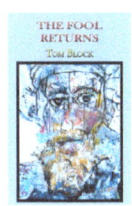
The Fool Returns
Tom Block
$20/$35, 250pp, 2014
ISBN: 978-1-68114-127-5

Third Law of Motion
Meg Files
$20/$35, 190pp, 2012
ISBN: 978-1-68114-169-5

Dancing in the Streets
Steven P. Unger
$20/$35, 208pp, 2012
ISBN: 978-1-68114-168-8

Blood Laws
Miguel Parga
$20/$35, 165pp, 2012
ISBN: 978-1-68114-161-9

Welcome Home, Sir
Steve Caplan
$15/$30, 154pp, 2011
ISBN: 978-1-68114-177-0

Eloquent Tattoo
Audrey Lavin
$15/$30, 162pp, 2012
ISBN: 978-1-68114-171-8

*The Private Side of a
Public Education*
Garry McGiboney
$15, 106pp, 2012, HC/PB
ISBN: 978-1-937536-19-0

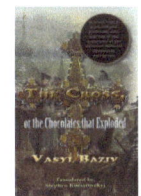
*The Cross, or The
Chocolates that Exploded*
Vasyl Baziv
$20/$35, 248pp, 2013
ISBN: 978-1-68114-144-2

ORDER FORM

All books in this catalog are available through **Ingram, YBP, Coutts Information Services, EBSCO, TotalBooX, ProQuest, Follett, Barnes and Noble, Amazon** and various other distribution channels. A variety of distributors are available to meet the needs of the majority of book buyers. Buyers can also order directly from Anaphora if they need 5 or more books to be shipped to a single location.

To make a purchase: e-mail the amount of books you need, the address where they should go, your preferred payment method (PayPal, SquareUp) and preferred discount percentage (20-55%). If you buy titles from Ingram, they come with a 40% distribution discount. Book shipments and printing speeds can be expedited at an extra cost, so please specify if you need the books in less than 2-3 weeks. Standard shipping for 5+ books is included in the price when shipping to US, UK, AU and CA. Shipping to other countries can take 6+ weeks and has varying costs.

Returns: Some of the books are refundable (check with Anaphora for details on specific titles). Most books are not returnable because books have to be destroyed and cannot be resold after a return. You can ask for the books you buy to be returnable, and for this the author would have to agree to take on any resulting losses.

For Reviewers: e-mail the publisher for free PDF or printed review copies of any books in this Catalog.

Mail or e-mail Orders To
(address is subject to change):
Anaphora Literary Press
Anna Faktorovich, Ph.D.
2419 Southdale Drive
Hephzibah, GA 30815

Contact With Questions/ Orders:
director@anaphoraliterary.com
1-470-289-6395 (12pm-9pm EST Mon-Sun)

ISBN-13: 978-1-523977-85-7
ISBN-10: 1-523977-85-X

QUANTITY	TITLE	COST
	SUBTOTAL	
Distribution Discount for orders of 5+ books: 20-55% depending on preference		
Shipping to US/UK/AU/CA for 5+ included Ask for shipping rates to other countries		
Expedited shipping and printing rates available upon request		
Optional Donation		
	TOTAL	

Checks, electronic banking transfers, SquareUp, and PayPal payments are accepted. Please fill out the information below and send the check to the address on the side bar. There is an extra 4% charge to use PayPal: e-mail the publisher for instructions.

Name: _____

Address: _____

City: _____ State: _____ Code: _____

Telephone: _____

E-Mail: _____